I have known Elmer Towns for the past 38 years, and he not only is faithful in church attendance, giving financially and serving at Thomas Road Baptist Church, but he has also performed just about every area of service for the church over the years. I can say from my lifelong experience that Elmer Towns loves the local church and serves God through the local church. If anyone knows *what is right with the church,* it is Elmer Towns; and he has expressed it perhaps better than anyone else.

Jonathan Falwell
Senior Pastor, Thomas Road Baptist Church,
Lynchburg, Virginia

Elmer Towns has been a friend to Christ Fellowship for many years. I have seen his love for the local church by example and have followed his ministry through the years. One of the reasons I chose to do my doctoral studies at Liberty Baptist Theological Seminary is because of Elmer Towns and his commitment to the church that Jesus established on this earth. I have learned so much about church growth because of his classes. Elmer Towns knows *what's right with the church.*

Tom Mullins
Senior Pastor, Christ Fellowship
Palm Beach Gardens, Florida

Now is the time for this book! And no one is more experienced to write it than Dr. Elmer Towns. I recently had the chance to speak in convocation at Liberty University. Of all the highlights from that visit to Liberty Mountain, it was the one hour I spent with my friend and mentor Dr. Towns that stands out! This book is like sitting down with Dr. Towns and having him teach you, inspire you and remind you why nothing is more important than the local church.

Nelson Searcy
Lead Pastor, The Journey Church of the City, New York City
Founder, www.ChurchLeaderInsights.com

My friend Elmer Towns is a gift to the church. He has always believed for and hoped for the best for the church, but in this volume he helps us to see what is going right in churches across the United States. Elmer Towns and this book are a gift to the church, and I am grateful for it.

Ed Stetzer
Author, *Compelled by Love* and *Comeback Churches*

Bestselling Author of *Fasting for Spiritual Breakthrough*

ELMER L. TOWNS

WHAT'S
Right with the
CHURCH

A Manifesto of Hope

Regal

From Gospel Light
Ventura, California, U.S.A.

Published by Regal
From Gospel Light
Ventura, California, U.S.A.
www.regalbooks.com
Printed in the U.S.A.

Library of Congress Cataloging-in-Publication Data
Towns, Elmer L.
What's right with the church : a manifesto of hope / Elmer Towns.
p. cm.
Includes bibliographical references and index.
ISBN 978-0-8307-5134-1 (hard cover : alk. paper)
1. Church. 2. Theology, Doctrinal—Popular works. I. Title.
BV600.3.T72 2009
262—dc22
2009021734

1 2 3 4 5 6 7 8 9 10 / 15 14 13 12 11 10 09

Rights for publishing this book outside the U.S.A. or in non-English languages are administered by Gospel Light Worldwide, an international not-for-profit ministry. For additional information, please visit www.glww.org, email info@glww.org, or write to Gospel Light Worldwide, 1957 Eastman Avenue, Ventura, CA 93003, U.S.A.

CONTENTS

WHAT'S RIGHT WITH THE CHURCH

From the beginning, the followers of Jesus Christ knew they were not just members of an organization, nor did they think they were an extension of Old Testament Judaism. They knew they were followers of the living Lord Jesus Christ. They had seen His resurrected body, had touched Him, eaten with Him and talked to Him. They knew they were members of a new thing—the church—His body, and that the church could transform the world.

The church is the most powerful transforming force in history. Yet outsiders love to make fun of the American church. They use glaring statistics to embarrass us, such as 35 percent of Christians get divorced, only 21 percent of Christians attend worship each week, and only five percent of Christian adults tithe.[1] And doesn't the media just love to juice up a story when a noted Christian falls into sin? When a leading evangelical leader was accused of a homosexual liaison, you would think the press was congregating over roadkill. And who hasn't heard about the problem of Roman Catholic clergy abusing young boys? Many people seem to enjoy a sneering laugh over church problems.

When a church is portrayed in a movie or on television, viewers get the impression that churches are either filled with wrinkled, white-headed old people, or hypocrites. And then there are those who like to attack the church's influence, accusing Christians of being mean-spirited or legalistic. Those on the outside don't understand the church and seem to always point out what's wrong with the church.

The fact that so many people misunderstand the church is reflective of the fact that the church is diverse in appearance. Observers are not sure if it is Republican, Democratic, members of a peace rally, an insurgent terrorist cell or a women's tea party!

We also get off-track in the area of "bigger and better." We live in an age in which surveys tell us who's leading in a political campaign and how many approve the President's job. And just about everything we purchase is driven by a statistical survey: 8 of 10 adults take this brand of sleeping pill at night; 65 percent of Americans eat this type of breakfast; more Americans drive such-and-such kind of car. So do not think it strange that we have surveys, median scores and case studies to determine the way churches should do ministry.

We're prone to take our cue from the 10 largest Sunday Schools or the 50 most influential churches. Christian record companies sign up Christian artists based on a Dove Award. And don't Christian bookstores give the most space on their shelves to the bestsellers and to the books that have been surveyed highest in sales? Christians listen to an author who has sold more *Purpose Driven* books than any other, and they read novels so they won't be *Left Behind;* that's because a Christian writer has sold more books in a series than any other author;

or they flock to hear a noted Christian speaker because he's on the bestselling list for the *Wall Street Journal*, *USA Today* and the *New York Times*.

All kinds of measuring devices influence Christianity. But when we measure the church, let's remember that's exactly what we are doing—we are measuring external things. Experts like to measure attendance, baptisms or how much money a church takes in, then use these statistics as an example of ministry to all other churches.

But beyond all the measuring and statistics, we must get back to the fact that the church is the Body of Jesus Christ (see Eph. 1:23-24). The church is Jesus on earth. What do we know about a body? It has life. The church is a living organism—a fact that elevates it above business and social organizations of our day. When we measure the outward things of the church, that's all we are doing. Externality is not the strength of Christianity. *What's Right with the Church* will look at the inward strength of the church. That's where you see what God is doing in the world.

I have traveled to all kinds of churches, studied them from all angles, and I can truly say that I love the church. I've given my life to serve the Lord through the church, even when I know she's not perfect. The church is like our children. We love our children when they get into mischief, because we have dreams for them; we know the wonderful things about them, and they have our blood running in their veins. But most of all, we love them because the Bible commands us to love them.

When you criticize the local church—the human organization—remember that its individual members can get bogged down in committees, do stupid things and be driven by their pride, prejudices and, yes, their sins. And when you praise the local church, remember that Christ works through its members who sacrifice their time, treasures and talents to serve other people. They experience the power of Christ who helps them overcome bad habits and selfish inclinations to live lives that exalt God.

I believe that young people who reject the contemporary American church would like its founder—Jesus Christ. He was as anti-bureaucratic as they come. He condemned the religious sham of His age, as today's young people condemn the religious sham of today's churches. Jesus was anti-bureaucratic in both His teachings and actions. In every sense of the word, Jesus was revolutionary.

The problem is, the revolution that Jesus began against the dead religion of His day has ultimately become—in many cases—a sham religion in our day. In many cases, the church is dead. The church of Jesus Christ should be as anti-institutional as Jesus was. That means that the church should be anti-establishment and revolutionary. The church as God's institution should challenge the sinful ways of man. The church should be the cutting edge of society. The church should be advocating a revolutionary religious way of life that transforms society, because that's what Jesus did. The church should lead in the fight against bureaucracy of all kinds and religious greed of every expression. But sometimes the church is an institution embroiled in bureaucracy and blinded by its wealth.

The fact that our young people misunderstand the church is reflective of the church's problem today. Like it or not, the outward church is a misunderstood institution. It is hypocritical in appearance, conflicting in focus and often ineffective in its ministry. As an institution it has organized itself by job descriptions and only moves forward on committee approval. That's why we don't know when we see a church on the street corner whether that church is fighting sin or is bogged down in its own infrastructure.

The church, however, was meant to do more than any other human organization, because Jesus told His followers to be mountain movers of barriers that block their way: "Say to this mountain, 'Move from here to there' and it will move" (Matt. 17:20, *NIV*). The church of Jesus Christ should be anti-institutional, anti-establishment and revolutionary. That's because the church is God's institution to challenge the sinful ways of man. As such, the church should be those Christians who form a more righteous way of life and transform the world.

Having said all that, this book is not about all the problems or sins of the church. Let someone else write that book.[2] This book will point out *what's right with the church*. This book is a manifesto of hope, for the church is the localized presence of Jesus Christ on earth. When Christians join together in the church, they can make a great impact on society. Each Christian, like each snowflake that falls from the sky, doesn't have much power in itself. But when enough snowflakes join together, they can cause your tires to spin or your car to skid on a snow-packed road, just as many Christians in a local church can turn around a crime-ridden community.

If you get enough snowflakes together, they can decree "no school, or no work," just as in the early 1900s when Christians banded together across America and voted "no manufacture or sale of alcoholic beverages anywhere in the United States."

Instead of criticizing the church, let's be strong individually and then band together with our fellow believers to make our churches strong to change our nation for God.

In Christ,
Elmer Towns
Written from my home at the foot of
the Blue Ridge Mountains

When the Church Is Right on Jesus

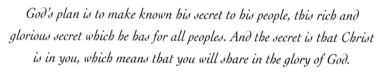

God's plan is to make known his secret to his people, this rich and glorious secret which he has for all peoples. And the secret is that Christ is in you, which means that you will share in the glory of God.

Colossians 1:27, *TEV*

Alexander, Caesar, Charlemagne, and myself founded empires; but what foundation did we rest the creations of our genius? Upon force. Jesus Christ founded an empire upon love; and at this hour millions of men would die for Him.

Napoleon Bonaparte

The name "Christianity" derives its name from "Christ" who is the foundation, focus and content of its existence. There is no Christianity if there is no supernatural Christ who died for the sins of the world and rose again to give His believers new life. When the church gets right on Jesus Christ, it is the most unique, transforming power in the world and the church that preaches Him becomes a revolutionary institution.

No other individual has impacted the history of civilization, in general, and Western civilization, in particular, than Jesus of Nazareth.

The name "Jesus" is among the most recognizable names in the world, whether He is worshiped by His followers or used as a curse word by those who deny Him or hate His convicting influence. But Jesus did not get His fame from a well-known family, nor did He become famous because of His birthplace. Jesus was born in an obscure village of Bethlehem in southern Palestine, in 4 B.C., to parents who were unknown outside that village.

Jesus was not a part of the religious ruling party of the state. The Pharisees rejected His message and continually sought to trip Him up and, in the end, they pressured Pilate to have Him crucified. Also, Jesus was a Jew—a hated ethnic minority that most of the other nations of the Roman Empire detested and persecuted. So what does this mean? Jesus was born to a persecuted people, and then, within that ethnic group, He was persecuted by the most rabid, rightwing sect among the Jews.

Jesus did not get fame by being born in Rome—the most powerful military empire to that date—to rule the world. Jesus grew up

14

in a society driven by Roman laws. He spoke their Latin language that held society together and lived under oppressive Roman laws, an unyielding force that ruled the world. As the Church began to grow, the Roman Empire became one of its chief persecutors. James the apostle was beheaded; the emperor Nero blamed the fire that gutted Rome in A.D. 66 on the Christians; then Peter was crucified upside down, and Paul was martyred.

According to *Foxe's Book of Martyrs*, some have estimated that there were at least 250,000 martyrs between A.D. 100 and 300. Whether His followers were thrown to the lions, crucified, stoned or dragged onto icy lakes to slowly freeze to death, Rome was the greatest persecutor of Jesus Christ. Yet, the influence of this one individual—Jesus—spread internally through the hearts of Roman citizens, eventually conquering the Empire when Constantine made Christianity a religion of Rome in A.D. 313.

The Church Is Not Just Doctrine

Many people don't understand Christianity, because they think it is primarily doctrinal beliefs, and to them, Christianity is nothing more than the Apostles' Creed or some other particular denominational statement. Perhaps they've been to a church where they've heard the Nicene Creed read, or they've heard the emphasis of some other doctrinal statement.

To those who see Christianity in dogmatic terms, they may think that Christianity is negative doctrine, that is, they don't believe in evolution, abortion, gay marriage or certain other dictates heard from the pulpit.

Still others believe that Christianity is a set of rules. Perhaps they have a friend who won't drink alcohol with them, or they've heard that Christians don't dance, use drugs, engage in premarital sex, nor will they use God's name as a curse word.

Some see Christianity as only a set of rules in which Christians express their faith solely by their refusal to watch pornography on the Internet, or their refusal to gamble in the office lottery, or their refusal to do other such things. Others describe their rigid focus by saying, "Christianity takes the fun out of life."

Still others wrongly interpret Christianity through only one worship practice they are familiar with, such as the Eucharist at a Roman Catholic church; or they've heard a wedding vow "to love, honor and obey" that turns them off; or they feel that Christianity is simply being quiet, meditative and behind stained-glass windows in a European cathedral. Perhaps they've been to a bombastic charismatic church where people shout, "Hallelujah!" dance in the Spirit or speak in tongues. They wrongly criticize Christianity on seeing one aspect of the church. They've missed the church's foundation—which is a Person—Jesus Christ.

But perhaps some have gone to the more expressive charismatic services that use a worship band with drums, a bass guitar, brass horns and a worship team of singers. They miss the choir, organ and piano, and wonder what's happening. They fail to scratch below the surface of what they see to find the real motive of worship, which is to honor and adore Jesus Christ.

In China today there are an estimated 120 million believers in Jesus Christ, all of this without denominational headquarters, mission boards, Sunday School literature or all of the other support organizations found in the American church. Chinese Christians meet in homes or other designated safe places for worship. They meet without the formality of traditional liturgical worship, most of the time without musical instruments and, for the most part, without trained clergy. How can a church this large and powerful not have Bible colleges and seminaries to train its ministers? The attraction is Jesus.

Yet the Chinese church sings its indigenous hymns to a different tune and beat than the American churches, and with a different schedule of worship from churches around the world. To those converted, the Chinese Christian church is simple: it's centered around a believer relating to Jesus Christ.

Perhaps Chinese Christianity is more vital than that which is found in the West. Why? Because they attach themselves to the core of Christianity; they know Jesus Christ and follow Him. They haven't added the barnacles that come with age—that have been attached to other churches in other nations.

In a godless communistic society, they have become obedient to Jesus. And should their godless government demand Christians to deny their faith, they would gladly become martyrs. Weekly, in the streets of the city or at work they share their faith with others because they know Christ and they feel that anyone who doesn't know Him will be lost for eternity. They risk persecution and imprisonment to share the most important thing in their life—Jesus.

What Made Jesus Distinctive?

What we know about Jesus is found primarily in the Gospels of Matthew, Mark, Luke and John. Jesus was called "the carpenter" (Mark 6:3). At a young age, His father died, and He then became the family breadwinner. He was raised in a home with only a mother, just as many children in the United States are today.

At age 30, He turned the family business over to His brothers and began preaching and teaching the message that the kingdom of heaven was coming. He walked daily among people, but they didn't recognize His greatness, nor did they know they were in the presence of deity: "He came to his own, and His own did not receive Him" (John 1:11). Jesus ministered itinerantly for approximately three and a half years.

Now, the universal influence of Christmas (His birth) and Easter (His death) is felt in commercial, political and educational realms. Most of the world even numbers its calendar by expressing time as B.C. (before Christ) and A.D. (after His birth).

The birth of Jesus is probably the most familiar aspect of Christianity that non-Christians know anything about. During the Christmas season, people see evidence of Christian worship that involves shepherds, wise men, a manger scene and a stable in Bethlehem. They exchange Christmas cards, attend seasonal Christmas services and are yearly reminded of the historical details surrounding the birth of Jesus Christ. But even then, the real meaning of Christmas does not penetrate below the surface of their hearts. But to the Christian, Jesus' supernatural conception by a virgin is the method whereby God became flesh and dwelt among us (see Isa. 7:14; John 1:14).

How Could the Eternal God
Take on Human Flesh?

Christian scholars answer that question by referring to the *kenosis*, a Greek word meaning emptying oneself. The apostle Paul used the term *kenosis* to describe how Jesus emptied Himself to become a man (see Phil. 2:7). In doing so, He veiled His glory, accepted the limitations of humanity and voluntarily gave up the independent use of His divine attributes.

When people saw Jesus walking among them, they didn't suspect that He was God, because His divine, sparkling glory was veiled. As a man, He became hungry, needed to sleep and was not whisked from one place to another by a miracle, but rather had to walk, sail in a boat or ride a donkey.

Why did Jesus willingly empty Himself and set aside all of the glory of heaven? Perhaps it was His love for mankind (see John 15:12) that He became a man and prepared to go to the cross to die for the sins of the world, even when the world continually rejected Him (see Rom. 5:8). Perhaps becoming a man was the best way to reveal the heavenly Father to us (see John 1:14,18; 14:7-11), but most of all, by becoming a man He provided salvation to overcome the sin of the world (see Rom. 5:11-21). "For God so loved the world that He gave His only begotten Son, that whoever believes in Him should not perish but have everlasting life" (John 3:16). Also, Jesus humbled Himself to the limitations of mere man and eventually yielded Himself to the sufferings of the cross, to give us an example that we should be humble in following Him (see Phil. 2:1-5).

Remember, God had promised to deliver the world through the seed of the woman (see Gen. 3:15). Also, Isaiah had predicted, "The virgin shall conceive and bear a Son, and shall call His name Immanuel" (Isa. 7:14). In the New Testament, Matthew 1:25, Luke 1:27 and Galatians 4:4 describe the virgin birth.

God used a virgin to introduce His Son into the world. Jesus was miraculously conceived in the Virgin Mary. The fact that He was born of a virgin doesn't mean that His birth was any different from anyone else's. Indeed, the delivery was a normal human birth; the miracle was the conception by the Holy Spirit in the womb of the Virgin Mary. That means that she had not sexually known any man.

Why? So that Jesus wouldn't be born with a sin nature like every other person born in the world. He lived without sin and then took our sin upon Himself to die in our place. So what does that mean? Jesus knew no sin (see 2 Cor. 5:21), was without sin (see Heb. 4:15), committed no sin (see 1 Pet. 2:22), and there was no sin found in Him (see 1 John 3:5).

When early Christian leaders tried to explain the human and divine nature of Jesus, they did so at the Council of Chalcedon, in A.D. 451. Then they issued the statement that Jesus was made "in two natures without confusion, without change, without division, without separation, the distinction of natures being by no means taken away by the union."[1]

Some later critics have claimed that the Council of Chalcedon is where the church made Jesus into God. But that conclusion is inconsistent with both the context and conclusion of the Council. The Council only wanted to write out the issues that had been historically believed by Christians from the first century. If they wanted, they could have declared His deity by denying His humanity. But they did not do that; they struggled with describing what Christians had always known about Jesus—that He was both God and man. Jesus was the God-Man.

How Did Jesus Grow?

Jesus was a perfect baby and child, and He developed in four areas: "And Jesus increased in wisdom and stature, and in favor with God and men" (Luke 2:52). First, Jesus grew in wisdom, meaning that He had to learn the things that any other person learns. Jesus had to learn a language, how to put together thoughts and develop understanding. Second, He increased in stature, meaning He had to eat to grow and remain healthy. Third, He grew spiritually, because it says He increased in favor with God; and finally, He grew socially when it describes Him as growing "in favor with God and men."

At age 30, John the Baptist baptized Jesus, even though John felt he was not worthy to do so (see Luke 3:23). "But Jesus answered and said to him, 'Permit it to be so now, for thus it is fitting for us to fulfill all righteousness'" (Matt. 3:15). In this act of baptism, Jesus identified with those who chose to follow Him, and He gave them an example of how they would identify with Him in the future when they joined a local church.

At the beginning of His ministry, Jesus fasted for 40 days and was hungry and vulnerable to temptation. Satan came to tempt Him on three occasions, described by Scripture as, "[He] was in all points tempted as we are, yet without sin" (Heb. 4:15). Jesus refused to make bread out of stones, He refused to give in to pride by casting Himself off a high place in the Temple so that angels could rescue Him, and He refused to worship Satan who promised to give Him the kingdoms of the earth.

Jesus Is God

At the beginning of His ministry, Jesus walked in obscurity across the dusty roads of Galilee, but eventually became one of the most well-known persons of all time. Today, He continues to walk across the pages of history, and many study

Him, examine Him and try to follow His example because they want to be outstanding Christians. There is probably more written about Jesus than any other person who ever lived.

If Jesus were not God, Christianity would not have become the powerful force in the world that it is today. The English poet Lord Byron said, "If ever a man was God, or God was man, Jesus was both."

When you look at the Jesus Christ of Scripture, you are studying one who claims to be God. Didn't He say, "He who has seen Me has seen the Father" (John 14:9)? And didn't He openly claim, "I and the Father are one" (John 10:30, *NIV*)?

But many say that He was not God, He was just a good man. But notice the inconsistency of that statement. If He were not God, then He would be a shameless imposter for claiming to be so. He would not be good. Jesus claimed to be God. But then Jesus would be worse than one who is simply not good; He would be a blasphemer because He claimed to be God.

Perhaps the greatest boast by Jesus is when He claimed to be the great "I AM" (John 8:58). The Old Testament word "LORD" is also translated "Jehovah" and is the primary name for deity in the Old Testament. The name "LORD" comes from the verb to be, "I AM," repeated twice. When Jesus called Himself the "I AM," He was referring to Himself as LORD.

Didn't Jesus say, "I am the bread of life" (John 6:35), "I am the light of the world" (John 8:12), "I am the door" (John 10:9), "I am the good shepherd" (John 10:11), "I am the resurrection and the life" (John 11:25) and "I am the way, the truth and the life" (John 14:6)? Jesus so infuriated the Jews by what He said that they constantly tried to kill Him. Remember, they charged Jesus with blasphemy before Pilate because He called Himself God.

The angel told Mary to call His name Jesus, which means "Jehovah Saves." Isaiah said, "'They shall call His name Immanuel,' which is translated, 'God with us'" (Matt. 1:23). Look at some of the other names of Jesus: Redeemer, Savior, Son of God, King, Cornerstone, Alpha and Omega, the Almighty. In all, there are more than 700 names, titles, metaphors and symbols to represent Jesus.[2] Why so many? Because Jesus is the God of the Ages, and it takes many names to describe who He is and what He does for us. Even then, we only get a small inkling of all that Jesus is.

The miracles of Jesus point to His deity. Some ask the question, "If God were to become flesh, what would He do?" God has to manifest Himself because God cannot hide Himself. It's only natural for God to do the miraculous, so it is only natural for Jesus to do miracles.

Listen to the blind man: "I was blind but now I see" (John 9:25, NIV). Listen to the leper who was cleansed by Jesus: "When he saw that he was healed, [he] returned, and with a loud voice glorified God, and fell down on his face at His feet, giving Him thanks" (Luke 17:15-16). Look at Lazarus, four days in the grave when he comes out of the tomb resurrected and ready to live again (see John 11:1-44). And then ask 5,000 people if they were fed with the miraculous bread and fish provided by Jesus (see John 6:1-14).

Finally, could any right-thinking person ever allow someone else to worship Him as God if He were not God? Jesus received worship: "And behold, a leper came and worshiped Him"

(Matt 8:2). Also, the very demons inside the demoniac of Gadara acknowledged the deity of Jesus (see Mark 5:6). After Jesus walked upon the water, and calmed the storms, His disciples worshiped Him (see Matt. 14:33). Who else can receive worship but God?

Wrap Up

The glue that holds Christian churches together is Jesus Christ. When any person becomes a Christian, he or she will receive Christ into his or her heart in conversion. Conversion is not learning about a historical person, as the Buddhist learns about the historical Buddha. Conversion is not being influenced by the thoughts or sayings of a past religious leader, as Islamists revere Muhammad. Conversion is not following the example of a selfless role model who died to be an example of humility.

No, conversion is none of the above. A sinner meets Christ, who is alive, because Christ was raised from the dead. Jesus sits at the right hand of God the Father in heaven. But in conversion, Christ actually enters the life of the newly converted believer at the moment of salvation. Paul described it this way: "I have been crucified with Christ: and I myself no longer live, but Christ lives in me. And the real life I now have within this body is a result of my trusting in the Son of God, who loved me and gave himself for me" (Gal. 2:20, *TLB*).

What's right with the church? Jesus.

WHEN THE CHURCH IS RIGHT ON THE BIBLE

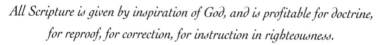

All Scripture is given by inspiration of God, and is profitable for doctrine, for reproof, for correction, for instruction in righteousness.

2 TIMOTHY 3:16

The Bible is the written Word of God, and because it is written it is confined and limited by the necessities of ink, and paper and leather. The voice of God however is alive and free as the sovereign God is free. "The words that I speak to you are spirit and life." The life is in the speaking words. God's Word in the Bible can have power only because it corresponds to God's Word in the universe. It is the present voice that makes the written voice powerful. Otherwise it would lie locked in slumber within the covers of a book.

A. W. TOZER, *THE PURSUIT OF GOD*

All of Christianity grows out of the unique collection of 66 books, written over 16 centuries, which today we call the Bible. It is more than history and doctrine. The Bible is the revelation of God, the message of salvation; and it has God's purpose and wonderful plan for us on this earth. The most uncaring "dude" can read its message and be transformed and potentially then become the next apostle Paul who transforms the culture in his world. Churches that get the Bible right are powerful institutions that can transform individuals.

Bob was a friend of mine in seminary. He gave a testimony one day of how the power of God was changing his life. Bob's father was anti-Christian, and by that I don't know if he was an atheist, denying the existence of God, or an agnostic, one who claims one cannot know that God exists. Bob said that every time his father was driving in the car and a sermon was heard on the radio, he would turn off the radio, beat on the dashboard vehemently and deny the truth of Christianity. If a magazine came into the home that described Christianity, Bob's father tore out the page and threw it away.

Bob attended one of the universities in greater Los Angeles, California, where he took a course in the literature of the world. In that class, he was assigned to read approximately 20 of the greatest books that had influenced history. As he surveyed the list of books, he reacted negatively to the Gospel of John from the Bible. Bob went to his professor, complaining, "I won't read this 'trash' from the Bible; it's only a myth."

"So are the Greek tragedies and the Roman myths," the teacher answered Bob, accusing him of being prejudiced and not having an open mind.

"But the Bible contains lies that mislead people," Bob argued.

"So does *Mein Kampf*, written by Adolph Hitler," the teacher reminded him. Then the teacher firmly suggested that Bob would have to read each book to determine the purpose of each writer then complete an essay on the thesis of each book, or not pass the course.

Bob was hit between the eyes with his bias and went back to his dorm room to find a Gideon New Testament that had been distributed by the Gideons on campus. Then, to make sure no one saw him, he locked the door and read carefully through the Gospel of John, taking notes, trying to formulate a statement that described why John wrote his Gospel.

The first time through he was looking for an intellectual analysis. Then he read it a second time out of curiosity and interest. He wanted to know why Jesus Christ had influenced people the way He did. The third time, Bob read the Gospel of John with his heart, not his head. He had to know more about the subject of the book, Jesus Christ. Then halfway through he knelt by his bed, looked open-eyed into heaven and prayed the thesis of the Gospel of John: "I believe."

The Bible transformed the life of my friend Bob, and he became a Bible expositor of a church in California. What the Bible did for Bob, it has done for millions who have honestly read the Bible and took its message at face value. The truth of Christianity is found in the Bible, and if there were no Bible, there would be no life-changing religion called Christianity.

The Bible is more than a history book that describes the Jewish people and the story of Jesus Christ. Christianity is more than doctrinal creeds to believe. Christianity is a Person—it is Jesus Christ—and we find the record of His life and sacrificial death in the Bible.

Christianity is more than rules, such as the Ten Commandments, so we don't read the Bible just to find principles or laws to follow. Something happens to readers who come to the Bible with an open mind, as the truth of God springs from the pages of the Bible, producing life. The Bible is life transforming.

The Bible contains stories, biographies, history, sermons and psalms that reflect the lives of real people doing real things, in a normal way. But then the Bible records how God intersected the lives of these people to make a difference in what they did or said. Today, some of God's people read the Bible to hear God speak to them. Other Christians read the Bible to find the will of God so they can do what God tells them to do, and serve Him. The Bible describes the people who lived by faith in the past and then tells how people today can exercise the same kind of faith.

The Bible contains stories of how God sent His servants, the prophets, to give a message to people. Sometimes this was a warning against disobeying God's commandments; at other times, the prophets gave directions on how God's people should live, or descriptions of how people should worship Him. Those who read the Bible today get the same message from God as those who originally heard it.

But the Bible is more than stories about God and His people. When you read the Bible, you are reading the actual words that

God put in it. The Bible was written by approximately 40 authors who were guided and empowered by the Holy Spirit so that what they wrote accurately reflected God's message.

When the Bible says, "All scripture is given by inspiration of God" (2 Tim. 3:16), the word "inspiration" means more than the power of an example, such as the reading of Shakespeare inspires the reader, or those listening to music are inspired by it. Inspiration means more. The word "inspiration" comes from two Greek words: *theo*, which means God, and *pneuma* which means life or breath. Therefore, when the authors were writing the Bible by inspiration, God breathed into them His words so that they wrote God's message using the words God gave to them. As each author chose words and put his ideas or thoughts into sentences, every word and every thought written down were God's words.

Because God inspired the words of the Bible, what you read in the Bible are words that have the "breath" of God in them. Therefore, when you read the words of the Bible, the actual Spirit of God is entering your life. Peter said to Jesus, "You have the words of eternal life" (John 6:68). The spoken words of Jesus and the written words of the Bible are both God's words. Because God is life, when you read and believe the words of the Bible, you get the very life of God in your soul. Then Jesus went on to explain, "The words that I speak to you are spirit, and they are life" (John 6:63). What does that mean? You get the Spirit of God and the life of God when you read the Bible; therefore, the Bible can transform your life by the life of God.

Remember, Jesus is called the Word of God: "In the beginning was the Word, and the Word was with God, and the Word was God" (John 1:1). That means that both Jesus and the Bible are called the Word of God. But there is a difference. Jesus is the *incarnate* Word because He was born of a virgin and came in the flesh so the human race could see what God was like. The Bible is the *inspired* Word of God written by God on pages so that humanity can read what God is like.

Therefore, both Jesus and the Bible are the Word of God. So, what does the Word do for us? The Word convicts of sin, exposes error, introduces people to God, tells of salvation and actually gives eternal life to those who read and believe its message.

The Bible is supernatural. Peter explained that a person was converted through the Bible: "Being born again . . . through the word of God" (1 Pet. 1:23). Therefore, we must do more than read the Bible to learn the accurate facts about what Jesus did and said on earth. We study the Bible to get more than just the contents of Christian doctrine. As we read and study the Bible, we must let its words become part of our life so that Christ may enter into our thinking and experience. As a result, we are born again and we receive the life of God.

The French philosopher Voltaire sat one day to rewrite Psalm 51 into a poem. Things were going well until he came to the statement: "Create in me a clean heart, O God" (Ps. 51:10). Though Voltaire was an agnostic and a chief opponent of Christianity in his day, fear gripped his heart when he attempted to understand and translate the truth of a "clean heart." As he wrote, a sudden terror of hell gripped him, and he tried to shake the feeling but found himself unable to write. Later, Voltaire confided to his friends that he could not go back and rethink that experience without an inner fear that continued to haunt him.

That experience suggests that the Bible is more than mere letters, symbols and words on paper. The Bible is a message from God that pierces the inner heart. The Bible is a revelation of God to people. When they see God and His holiness, they see their sin. When we understand the work of Scripture in a person's heart, we begin to understand the unique power of the Bible.

Because God is who He is, and He wrote the Bible, then what is true of God must be characterized in His book. Therefore, a holy God wrote a holy book. A life-changing God wrote a life-changing book. An all-knowing God wrote a book that knows our inner recesses. A saving God wrote a book that has a message of salvation. And an eternal God wrote a book that will give us eternal life. God is the source of the Bible (see Deut. 29:29); Christ is the central theme of the Bible (see John 5:38); and the Holy Spirit is the divine author of Scripture (see 2 Pet. 1:20-21). Didn't Jesus describe the Bible as "every word that proceeds from the mouth of God" (Matt. 4:4)?

The phrase "dual authors" means that there were two sources who wrote the Bible—men and the Holy Spirit. Therefore, the Bible is a human book with different journalistic expressions and different vocabulary (Paul used a legal vocabulary, while Luke used a medical vocabulary). The Bible was written by humans, yet the Holy Spirit guaranteed its accuracy and word selection.

The dual authorship of more than 40 men who wrote the Holy Scriptures makes the Bible an even more unique book. It was written over a period of 1,600 years (a collection of letters, sermons, poems, history, stories), yet it has a single theme. Some writers were scholars, such as Moses and Paul, who probably received the finest education of their day. Other writers raised cattle or sheep, while others were fishermen; and there was one who was a tax collector, considered a disgraceful occupation of its day. With more than 40 different writers from various backgrounds, it is miraculous that they produced a single book with a harmonious theme and a single purpose.

Also, consider that the Bible was written on two continents and in 12 different nations, over a period of 1,600 years; yet, when you read the Bible, you get the impression that there was only one author of the whole.

Preaching the Whole Bible

Chuck Smith of Calvary Chapel, Costa Mesa, California, preaches through the Bible verse by verse.[1] He begins at Genesis 1:1 and covers every chapter and verse until he arrives at Revelation 22:21. It is out of his deep conviction that he preaches expositionally through the Bible.

Joe Focht, pastor of Calvary Chapel in greater Philadelphia, Pennsylvania, was an unsaved "hippie" who was greatly influenced by Chuck Smith after he got saved.[2] While in the church, Chuck Smith completed his study through the entire Bible and that evening announced that he would begin preaching the next Sunday at Genesis 1:1. The following Sunday, Smith announced to the congregation, "Today's sermon begins at Genesis 1:1." Joe Focht punched his buddy and said, "Hang on, this will be a long sermon. Smith preaches through the Bible about every four years."

Smith was a Pentecostal preacher for 17 years before beginning Calvary Chapel in Costa Mesa. He confesses that during that time he was a topical preacher. Yet, when he began the first Calvary Chapel, he committed to preach through the entire Bible verse by verse. The power of the Word had changed him and his church.

Smith, by vowing to teach the Word of God to his congregation in such a fashion, recognized the need to incorporate the whole of the Bible into his teaching sermons. Potential converts would undoubtedly have many questions about the Christian faith that would be hard for Smith's evangelical team to answer without a thorough knowledge of the gospel.[3]

Furthermore, Smith wanted to hold to the teachings of Paul the apostle as put forth in Acts 20:27: "For I [Paul] have not shunned to declare to you the whole counsel of God." In Smith's eyes, "The only way a person could make that claim to his congregation would be if he taught through the whole Word of God with them, from Genesis to Revelation."[4] Therefore, Smith instituted a strict regimen of weekly Bible teaching at Calvary Chapel, usually consisting of about 10 chapters of Scripture per week (Sunday and Wednesday), starting at Genesis 1:1 and continuing through the rest of the Bible until the last word of the book of Revelation.[5]

Of all the evangelical seminaries, Dallas Theological Seminary is best known for producing expositional preachers; that is, those with a strong Bible-teaching ministry. Whereas many evangelical seminaries are known for producing ministers with various approaches to ministry, Dallas focuses on preparing expositors. Posted high on the wall of the chapel for all students to see is the seminary's seal with the words, κηρυξον τον λογον. Because we all had four years of Greek, we knew that it challenged us to preach the Word (see 2 Tim. 4:2). Dr. Lewis Sperry Chafer, founder of Dallas Theological

Seminary, announced on many occasions to the students, "You haven't preached the gospel until you've given the people something to believe."

I am a Dallas graduate, and I love to teach the Scriptures verse by verse. However, I backed into this approach. In college, at the age of 19, I began pastoring the Westminster Presbyterian Church of Savannah, Georgia, preaching two sermons each weekend. I knew nothing about the different styles of preaching or anything about worship styles (see chapter 6). Each weekend, I preached the hottest sermon I had heard the previous week in chapel. Sometimes I heard something outstanding in a Bible class, so I preached that the next Sunday.

Then came summer vacation, when my sermon source dried up. There were no college chapels to give me ideas for sermons. I found a book of sermons at a local Christian bookstore and preached the good ones, but they also dried up. I remembered a Bible exegetical class where we studied verse by verse the book of Ephesians. So I began "teaching" Ephesians, and the people loved it, perhaps better than my "sensationally hot" sermons. When I saw what Ephesians did to the congregation, I continued the verse-by-verse method through 1 Peter. Upon arriving at Dallas Theological Seminary, they reinforced how I was already preaching.

Bible-expositional churches follow the watchword of the reformers in the 1500s: *sola scriptura,* "scripture alone." But they feel the reformers did not go far enough. They believe that like the reformers their messages must be based in the Scriptures, but they also must be preached from the Scriptures. Their focus is the Scriptures as they explain the Scriptures.

Michael R. Tucker, a graduate of Conservative Baptist Seminary, cites the definition of expositional preaching by Haddon Robinson, former president of Conservative Baptist Seminary, to explain his approach to preaching:

> The proclamation of a biblical concept derived from an historical-grammatical study of a passage in its context which the Holy Spirit has first made vital in the personality of the preacher and through him applies accurately in the experience of the congregation.[6]

Those who are expositional preachers do so out of deep conviction that this is what God wants them to do. But more importantly, verse-by-verse preaching will get more results than anything else. Gary Inrig, pastor of Bethel Chapel in Calgary, Alberta, Canada, said:

> The complete and consecutive teaching of Scripture must receive a very high priority in assembly life. Nothing is more beneficial than a ministry of expository preaching which covers the sweep of all the books of the Bible. . . . Expository preaching will keep solid food before believers and bring a balanced and nutritious diet. . . . Only God's Word quickened by His Spirit can establish believers and make them strong in Christ, and so all of our church services focus upon the teaching of Scripture.[7]

When you hear a sermon in a Bible expositional church, it is probably more the exercise of the spiritual gift of teaching than the spiritual gift of exhortation. That means the expositional pastor is going to spend more time studying the Scriptures to find out what the Bible means and prepare Bible content for his teaching ministry. John MacArthur, pastor of Grace Community Church in Sun Valley, California, says he spends 30 hours a week studying the Scriptures in preparation for his sermons.[8]

Most Bible expositors do not give an invitation at the end of their sermon. The emphasis of a Bible expositional church is "thou shalt know the Scriptures," while the emphasis of an evangelistic church is "thou shalt come to Christ." Yet the Bible expositional preachers believe in evangelism. Tucker says that most evangelism takes place outside the church building and that preaching services are primarily for the maturing of the Saints. He goes on to say that if Christians are built up in the faith through the teaching of the Word of God, then they are equipped to go out and do the work of ministry in their daily lives.[9]

Dan Baumann, former pastor of Whittier Area Baptist Fellowship Church in Whittier, California, stated, "By their definition, the church is *not* primarily a soul-winning station, a forum for contemporary issues, or a showcase for music and/or drama; it is a schoolhouse for the training of Christians."[10]

The Most Influential Book in History

Because followers of Jesus know the power of the Bible, they have taken God's Word to every civilization to preach the message "Jesus Saves." Immediately after getting people to know Jesus, missionaries have attempted to translate the Bible into the language of the people so the people could hear sermons and lessons in their own language and dialect. Then missionaries taught the people to read so they could read the message of the Bible for themselves.

This is a deep passion of the Christian church today as missionaries continue to translate the Bible into every foreign language in the civilized world. There remain approximately a thousand languages to go, and today there are about 200 million (uncivilized) people who do not have the Bible in their own language.[11]

When the Bible has been translated into the language of uncivilized tribes, individuals become converted to Christianity and slowly the tribe becomes civilized. Missionaries from organizations such as Wycliffe Bible Translators have gone into heathen tribes, learned their language and reduced it into letters, words and sentences.[12] Then they have translated the Bible into the language of the people and taught them to read the Bible. When member after member of a heathen tribe has heard the Bible and made it a part of their life, they want a better life. This is technically called *redemption and lift:* When God redeems people, He lifts them to a higher level of civilization. Eventually the Bible civilizes a tribe so that they live on a higher level than before. Wherever the Bible goes, culture and civilization shortly follow.

Some of the greatest leaders in the world have appreciated the influence of the Bible. John Adams wrote an entry in his diary on February 22, 1756:

Suppose a nation in some distant region should take the Bible for their only law book, and every member

37

should regulate his conduct by the precepts there contained! Every member would be obliged in conscience to temperance, frugality and industry: to justice, kindness and charity towards his fellow men: and to piety, love and reverence toward Almighty God. . . . What a Eutopia, what a Paradise would this region be.

The Bible has been one of the greatest motivators to the good of those who believe its contents. Christian leaders have lived by the Bible, taught the Bible and given their lives to master the Bible. No other religion has produced as many books to explain itself, or more beautiful paintings and works of art to express the message of the Bible, or more music to reflect the emotions and message of God's Word. All that influence comes from the message of the Bible.

The Greatness of the Bible

The Bible is a great book because it tells the truth about the sinfulness of man. It teaches that no matter how good anyone is outwardly, he is a sinner and falls short of God's standards. At the end of his life, the apostle Paul could testify to his own sinfulness: "Christ Jesus came into the world to save sinners, of whom I am chief" (1 Tim. 1:15).

The Bible never flinches to tell the bad news about good men. It tells of how Abraham, the man of faith, couldn't trust God, so he lied. It tells how David, a man after God's own heart, committed adultery with Bathsheba. It tells how Peter, the bold fisherman, denied Jesus three times and cursed. The list could go on because the Bible tells the truth about the faults of God's leaders. Yet, the average reader doesn't read about the sin of Noah—getting drunk—and then go out to do the same. Nor do they read about Solomon's many wives and follow his example. No, the Bible is a truthful book that looks beyond the sins of its people to the truth it upholds (see Gen. 9:20-23; 20; 2 Sam. 11; 1 Kings 11; Mark 14:16-72).

Perhaps the greatest influence of the Bible is its convicting, convincing, converting power to all who honestly accept its message and believe in Jesus Christ. I was a normal high school student who cussed as much as the average guy. I told lies to keep out of trouble. In my heart I fully admitted that I lied, because normal people can't lie to themselves. I had immoral thoughts and a vicious temper. Yet the Bible *convicted* me of my sin, and *convinced* me to seek Jesus Christ as Savior, and *converted* me when I asked Jesus to come into my heart.[13]

What were the results of my conversion? God transformed my mouth; I no longer spoke curses. I began memorizing Scripture that changed my desires about sin, and I had an overwhelming desire to serve God.

Finally, the Bible is a story of present hope for those who are discouraged, despondent or have no purpose in life. The Bible tells that God loves you and has a wonderful plan for your life. The Bible is the story of the future when Christ will return to rapture His people to be with Him. When we die, our bodies will be resurrected, and we will live with God for all eternity (see chapter 11 for the details).

Just as you can't have Christianity without a person—without Jesus Christ—so you can't have Christianity without a book—the Bible. What is right with the church? The Bible is right.

WHEN THE CHURCH IS RIGHT ON CONVERSION

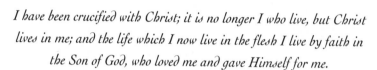

I have been crucified with Christ; it is no longer I who live, but Christ lives in me; and the life which I now live in the flesh I live by faith in the Son of God, who loved me and gave Himself for me.

GALATIANS 2:20

Conversion is the act of joining our hands to the pierced hand of the crucified Savior. The new life begins with the taking of Christ's hand, and His taking hold, in infinite love, of our weak hands.

THEODORE LEDYARD CUYLER

Palaces and pyramids are reared by laying one brick or block at a time; and the Kingdom of Christ is enlarged by individual conversions.

JAMES H. AUGHEY

Unlike all other religions of the world, and modern Universalists, Jesus boldly proclaimed that He was the exclusive way to God. The heart of Christianity is personal forgiveness of sins because Christ died, was buried and on the third day rose from the dead to give transforming life to those who believe in Him. Churches that get salvation right give people a wonderful basis for life on this earth and a hope for life beyond the grave.

The Bible records Jesus saying that He is the exclusive way to God: "I am the way, the truth, and the life. No one comes to the Father except through Me" (John 14:6). When Jesus said, "No one [man]," it excluded any other way to God or heaven.

In January 2009, I said that we should pray for the conversion of Barack Obama, president of the United States, because he was not saved. Many people were shocked that I would say such a harsh thing. But when Rick Warren interviewed Barack Obama while campaigning for the presidency on a television program called "The Civil Forum on the Presidency," a venue of the back-to-back interviews of U. S. presidential candidates John McCain and Barack Obama, he asked, "Is Jesus Christ the only way to heaven?" Obama answered, "There are many other ways to heaven, including the Muslims, the Jews and other religions."

When people were repelled by my statement that Obama was not a Christian, I answered that the very nature of coming to Jesus for salvation was so totally absorbing, that those who thought otherwise had not really come to Christ. If one doesn't understand the exclusive demands of Jesus Christ, then that person has not applied the exclusive demands of Jesus to his or her life. Other religions demand that their doctrine or their way of life or their good works must be followed to obtain salvation. But none of these are Christianity.

Christianity is a Person—Jesus Christ; and to be saved, you must be in right relationship to Jesus Christ. When a person becomes saved, he forms a life-long relationship with Jesus Christ, and learns the conditions He set: "If anyone desires to come after Me, let him deny himself, and take up his cross daily, and follow Me" (Luke 9:23).

To be saved, you cannot try Jesus Christ, like a person tasting all the pies at a baking contest. To meet Jesus Christ in salvation is not like a young man dating all the other girls at school. No! Salvation is choosing Christ and saying no to all the others. When a person becomes a Christian, he looks at Jesus Christ and Him alone for salvation and then testifies, "For to me, to live is Christ" (Phil. 1:21).

My Conversion

My mother met my father at a dance in the late 1920s, and they married in 1930. I was born two years later. As a little child, I was dragged to the taverns and speakeasies around Savannah, Georgia. It was the day of prohibition, and my mother always carried the liquor bottle in her purse because she did not want revenuers to arrest my father. I would not have found salvation in that family, so I don't attribute my conversion to my home life (my father died an alcoholic).

In 1938, Jimmy Breland, a door-to-door coffee salesman, was trying to sell my mother Jewel Tea Coffee when I came into the living room.

"Where do you go to Sunday School?" Jimmy asked me.

"What's Sunday School?" I innocently asked.

Jimmy went on to tell me that it was a place where they sang songs, told Bible stories, colored in books . . . and then he described the sand table where we could fashion mountains just like those in the Holy Land where Jesus walked. Then he told me they would place a mirror in the sand, and he walked his fingers like a man walking across a lake to tell me that Jesus walked on the lake. I interrupted, "Like walking across the Savannah River?"

The sand table hooked me; I really wanted to go to Sunday School, and Jimmy negotiated with my mother to pick me up when I was old enough to attend regular school. Once I started, my mother wanted me to be sophisticated like the people who lived in that section of town. I had to go every Sunday to get a perfect attendance pin, followed by a second year with a wreath, and a third, a bar; and another bar each year thereafter.[1]

Jimmy was an outstanding teacher, and I memorized Bible verses. He loved lists. I had to memorize lists of the 12 disciples, the books of the Bible, the days of creation, the 12 tribes of Israel and any other list we happened across. I memorized a weekly Bible verse, and I knew about Jesus Christ and said on many occasions that I believed in Him.

On Easter Sunday 1944, when I was 12 years old, I sat in the church membership class with about 12 other young people from the church. We were sitting in a circle where the pastor asked each one of us a question and then turned to the rest of the group and said, "Do you believe that?"

Each time, I nodded my head yes.

The question directed to me was, "Do you believe in the virgin birth?" In those days, we were more naïve about sexual matters than today, and I was not sure what the virgin birth was. But if the church taught it, I agreed with it and said, "Yes, sir."

The last boy in the circle was Frank Perry, who was asked, "Do you believe that Jesus Christ is coming back to earth?" He said, "Yes, sir." And then the pastor asked the rest of us if we agreed. "Yes, sir," I said out loud and shook my head yes, but in my heart I knew I was not ready should He come. I knew I would be lost if Jesus Christ returned to earth.

Every afternoon, I delivered newspapers on my bicycle for spending money. On several occasions, I thought about salvation and would cry out, "God, save me!" On other occasions, I prayed, "Come into my heart and save me." But in my heart, I knew that I was not saved after I prayed those words.

Somewhere in grade school, I picked up a bad habit of cursing and knew it was wrong. When I was around nine years old, I went to Presbyterian Youth Fellowship, where a candle was placed on the table in front of the room alongside a small empty bowl. We were given a small piece of paper—about three times the size of a fortune cookie—and were told to write our sins on the piece of paper. I wrote the word "cursing," crumbled up the paper and put it in the bowl. The lady touched the pieces of paper with a candle, and I inwardly thought God allowed my cursing to go up in flames. But my cursing came back.

A little while later, we had the same experience. There was a candle and a bowl, and again they passed out those small sheets of paper. This time I didn't write the word "cursing" but I wrote each curse word I remembered, saying I honestly wanted to quit cursing because I knew it displeased God. When the candle was touched to all the papers, again I said, "God, there goes my cursing." But again, my cursing returned.

About my junior year in high school, I went to Presbyterian youth camp and attended a big bonfire service on the last night. Several young people went forward, took a small chip of wood, gave a testimony and threw their chip into the fire. We were told that we added our light to a larger light that could influence the world.

When I went forward, I found a chip of wood that had been splattered with mud. I held it up and dramatically said, "The dirt on this chip of wood represents my dirty tongue." Before all the young people, I made a dramatic pledge of repentance to never curse again. I threw my chip into the fire.

I was able to keep my commitment for approximately two weeks. While working on my paper delivery route, my stack of newspapers was bundled with wire that I received each afternoon. I would bend the wire back and forth to break it. That particular afternoon, a jagged edge popped loose, suddenly gashing my knuckle. Blood gushed out and I cursed the paper. My good friend Art Winn reminded me that I had promised never to curse again, so I cursed him. I don't know if I was mad at the wire or mad at my inability to keep my promise. But I remember cursing several things that afternoon. I realized I couldn't quit cursing, so I didn't try again.

In July 1950, I had just graduated from high school and was planning on attending Armstrong State University (it was only a junior college at that time). Bill and Burt Harding, twin brothers who were students at Columbia Bible College, were pastoring Bonna Bella Presbyterian Church near Savannah, Georgia. Later, I found out they were leading a prayer meeting early every morning where they called my name before God and asked for my conversion.

Joel Ortendahl, another student from Columbia Bible College, held a revival meeting at the church in the third week of July. Each evening, several people came forward for conversion. It was an extraordinary time. People were getting saved that no one expected to see saved. People sensed the presence of God in those meetings.

On July 25, no one went forward, and Bill Harding stood by the communion table to say, "Someone is here who should have come forward tonight. You know who you are, but you were afraid or ashamed to come forward." I knew he was talking about me. Bill continued, "You're holding on to that pew and won't let go." I looked down and saw my knuckles firmly hanging on. Like the sensation of picking up something hot, I quickly let go. Bill said, "Go home, kneel by your bed, look into heaven and pray, 'Lord, I've never done this before; Jesus, come into my heart and save me.'"

When I got home, I determined to say that prayer; so I knelt by my bed. I realized I had prayed many times, "Jesus come into my heart," but it never worked. So I refused to say it again, but prayed the Lord's Prayer and got in bed and tried to go to sleep. Instead, I tossed and turned, then rationalized that I ought to try the prayer. As I knelt, I again rationalized that I had prayed these words so many times. I did not realize that a human soul was struggling with life or death, and behind the scenes, God the Father and Satan were struggling for my soul.

So the second time, I prayed, "Now I lay me down to sleep, I pray the Lord my soul to keep . . ." Again I got in bed, but again I couldn't sleep.

The third time I got out of bed and did as Bill directed. I looked to heaven and said, "Lord, I've never done this before . . ."

When I admitted that I was lost, for about three or four seconds I felt the horrors of hell, as if I were already there. Then, like a drowning man grabbing a rope, I looked towards heaven and prayed, "Jesus, come into my heart and save me."

With that simple prayer, I was gripped with the conviction that Jesus came into my heart, that I was saved and I knew it for sure. I jumped up, and with a fist pump, I began singing, "Amazing grace how sweet the sound that saved a wretch like me, I once was lost but now am found, was blind but now I see." With that last phrase of the song, I realized

> The testimony of my conversion is given to illustrate the experience of many millions who have had a similar experience when meeting Jesus Christ. The issues that brought us to Christ were different, including differences of age, place, maturity and sin that drew us to seek salvation. But there is a sameness in each story. We knew we were lost, we met a Person—Jesus Christ—and He forgave us our sin and changed our lives forever.

that I had been blind to salvation. That night, for the first time in my life, I saw the light of Jesus Christ.

One of the most amazing facts is that I never cursed again. When I was saved, I didn't tell God I was sorry for cursing, although I was sorry for all of my sins. I didn't ask God to help me quit cursing. I just met a person, Jesus Christ, and He transformed my life. Obviously, joining the church didn't change my life; and many people wrongly think that Christianity equals joining the church or ascribing to a set of doctrines or even living by a set of standards.

What Is Conversion?

My salvation was a *conversion*. Conversion simply means to turn from sin (to repent) and completely turn to Jesus Christ (exercise faith for salvation).

"Conversion" is one of the most misunderstood of all religious terms. Technically, "conversion" is a human term used by many groups other than Christians. When the movie star Elizabeth Taylor prepared to marry the pop singer Eddie Fisher, who was Jewish, she converted to the Jewish faith. When Cassius Clay (who now calls himself Muhammad Ali) was the heavyweight champion of the world, he converted to the Muslim faith. The dictionary says that conversion is "change in character, form, or function."[2]

In football, conversion is the extra point after a touchdown, suggesting additional points. In mathematics, conversion is a mathematical expression to clear fractions. And of course, many other religions use the term "conversion" to adopt their religion, whether used in Buddhism, Confucianism, Hinduism or Baha'i.

According to the Bible, conversion is a voluntary change of the mind, emotions and will as the person turns from sin to faith in Christ as Savior. But notice that conversion is human activity.

When you think of conversion, it is one door with two sides. One side of the door is human activity, what man does, which involves the intellect, emotions and will. The other side of the door is God's activity, which is regeneration whereby God transforms people, gives them new desires, new life and makes them a part of His family. Regeneration is what God does in contrast to conversion, which is what man does.

As I've already stated, conversion involves three parts—intellect, emotion and will, which is a definition of personality, i.e., a person's personality is made up of intellect, emotion, will, self-perception and self-direction. So, conversion involves the total person, responding totally to God.

The first part is the mind or intellect, so you must know that you are a sinner before God: "For all have sinned and fall short of the glory of God" (Rom. 3:23). That means they realize they are under the punishment of God for their sins, i.e., "the wages of sin is death" (Rom. 6:23). After you know that punishment awaits you, you must realize that Christ took your punishment: "God demonstrates His love toward us, in that while we were yet sinners, Christ died for us" (Rom. 5:8).

But knowing all these facts does not save a person, nor does it enable him to push the door open into heaven. Jesus realized that many would have head knowledge but not heart knowledge when He said, "Not everyone who says to Me, 'Lord, Lord,' shall enter the kingdom of heaven, but he who does the will of My Father in heaven" (Matt. 7:21). Therefore, a person can't learn his or her way into heaven by doing anything like memorizing the catechism or attending a church membership class.

The second aspect of conversion involves feeling or emotion. Most of the time our emotions motivate us to turn to God. As Paul said, "Your sorrow led to repentance" (2 Cor. 7:9). Paul continues describing what it takes to get a person converted: "For godly sorrow produces repentance leading to salvation" (2 Cor. 7:10). A person may weep, be depressed or feel guilt because of his sin, but these emotions never get a person saved, they only motivate someone to turn to Christ who can save him.

There's a difference between being sorry for sin and being sorry that you were caught. There have been many people who have been caught lying and who have become embarrassed, but they were not sorry because they lied; they were sorry they got caught lying.

I once had an employee who was skipping work, and when I confronted him with his absences he wrote me an email suggesting, "I'm sorry that I made you mad." My reaction was not the issue. He should have said, "I'm sorry for missing work." In the same way, when we sin against the God of the universe, we should be sorry that we have offended God, not that we were caught sinning. "The sorrow of the world produces death" (2 Cor. 7:10). Therefore, not everyone who weeps at the altar is in fact converted. Salvation is more than weeping over sin.

The third aspect of conversion is an expression of the volition or will. This is why Peter said, "Repent therefore and be converted" (Acts 3:19). Repentance is an act of the will whereby we strongly choose to quit sinning.

In summary, we must know God's plan of salvation, but knowledge never saved anyone. Our emotions must be effected, but an emotional conversion alone will never get anyone into heaven. And we must make a choice for God. But if our choice is not based on proper knowledge, it is ineffective. Hence, all three—intellect, emotions and will—become operative in conversion when a person expresses faith in Jesus Christ as his or her Savior.

Faith Experience

Faith in Jesus Christ is very simple yet complex. Faith is as simple as a drowning man grabbing for a life preserver or the thief on the cross who said, "Remember me when You come into Your kingdom" (Luke 23:42). That simple statement of faith—calling Jesus Lord—was effective because Jesus said, "Today you will be with Me in paradise" (Luke 23:43).

Faith is more than head knowledge, for if faith were head knowledge alone, then the devils could be saved, because the Bible says, "the demons believe—and tremble" (Jas. 2:19). Remember, faith is not doing something for God; faith is your relationship with God. You accept Christ as Savior, and He comes into your heart: "But as many as received Him, to them He gave the right to become children of God, to those who believe in His name" (John 1:12).

Salvation is not about doing good works for God, because good works cannot save you. Jesus said, "Many will say to Me in that day, 'Lord, Lord, have we not prophesied in Your name . . . and done many wonders in Your name?'" (Matt. 7:22). Jesus answers those who do good works, "I never knew you" (Matt. 7:23).

"Faith" is a noun that describes the content of our belief; "believe" is a verb that describes our putting trust in Jesus Christ to save us. When Paul was beaten and thrown in a prison in

Philippi, God sent a great earthquake in the middle of the night, and the jailor came running into the midst of his prisoners thinking they had escaped. He was going to commit suicide rather than face his superiors. Paul told him that all the prisoners were still there. It's then that the jailor asked the eternal question, "What must I do to be saved?" (Acts 16:30).

Paul's answer was very simple then, and it's the same answer to everyone today: "Believe on the Lord Jesus Christ, and you will be saved" (Acts 16:31). Believing in Jesus involves both the heart and the will. When the Ethiopian eunuch wanted Christian baptism, Philip told him, "Believe with all your heart" (Acts 8:37). Obviously, to "believe with all your heart" involves all of one's total knowledge, feeling and choice of God.

Experience Regeneration

Let's go back to the door we discussed earlier. The human side of the door is called conversion—what a man, woman or child must do. God's side of the door is called regeneration, which is what only God can do.

The term "regeneration" is the biblical term for being *born again*. Jesus met Nicodemus, a religious ruler in Jerusalem, at night. When Nicodemus tried to flatter Jesus by complimenting His many miracles, Jesus told him bluntly, "Unless one is born again, he cannot see the kingdom of God" (John 3:3).

Nicodemus had one of the best educations in Jerusalem, but knowledge was not enough. Nicodemus served God as a religious leader, but life actions were not enough. Even if he had an outwardly holy life, just keeping the rules was not enough. Nicodemus had to be born again.

When one is born again, it means there has been a change of the heart wrought by God so that a person is transformed from darkness to light. How is one born again? Jesus said it happens when one is "born of the Spirit" (John 3:6). It is what the Holy Spirit does in your heart.

So how does a person experience the new birth? It starts with the head. "Whosoever believes that Jesus is the Christ is born of God" (1 John 5:1). And how does that happen? A person must meet Jesus Christ. John explains, "But as many as received Him [Christ] . . . were born . . . of God" (John 1:12-13).

When people are born again, they are transformed so that they don't want to continue living in sin. The Bible says, "We know that whoever is born of God does not sin; but who has been born of God keeps himself" (1 John 5:18). What does the Bible mean when it says, "does not sin"? The word "sin" is in the continuous tense, meaning that if you are born again, you do not *continually* sin, but you keep yourself from sin.

When I was born again on July 20, 1950, the following Saturday I knew my life was changed. All through high school I goofed off and almost never took a book home. I used study halls for homework and spent my afternoons delivering papers and my evenings going to movies.

When the Saturday newspaper came, the first thing I did was open to the movie page and plan my week by the movies I would attend. On some evenings, I went to two movies so I could see all the new ones shown that week. But after I was born again, I first turned to the church page on Saturdays and planned out my week by the revivals I would attend. One night I went to the Baptist church, another night to the Pentecostal and another night to the Christian and Missionary Alliance church. I no longer wanted to go to movies; I wanted to be where the Word of God was preached, where people were being saved and where I could feel the presence of God. God had transformed my attitude.

When you are born again, you receive a new nature from God: "Therefore, if any man is in Christ, he is a new creation; old things are passed away; behold, all things have become new" (2 Cor. 5:17). You're still tempted to do wrong, and sometimes you fail. But the issue is not whether you're perfect; the issue is doing God's will and pleasing Him. All of us sin (see 1 John 1:8,10) and all of us should come daily to ask God's forgiveness (see 1 John 1:9). But you have surrendered to Jesus Christ and you daily tell the old nature, "No!" The greatest proof that you have been saved is your new nature, with its new desires, new strength and a new purpose in life.

Conversion-focused Churches

A church is right when it's right on conversion. There are many churches that are known for their soul-winning purpose. They exhort their members to attend evangelistic visitation where they intentionally go out to win people to Christ. They are characterized by preaching the gospel to get people saved in prisons, nursing homes and other public gatherings. They end their church services with a gospel invitation where people are exhorted to come forward and receive Christ, much like a Billy Graham evangelistic crusade.

Some seeker churches are focused on reaching unsaved people, although they don't give an invitation, nor do they plan evangelistic activities. Bill Hybels, father of the seeker movement, was in a conference with me in San Diego when his church first gained national attention. Hybels said he didn't want to use traditional church music that turned off the new seeker generation. He said the same of traditional sermons, and he wanted his church to look like a civic center so that unsaved seekers would be comfortable and listen to the gospel. His church, Willow Creek Community Church, in South Barrington, Illinois, is one of the great churches in America where many people still find Christ.

The late D. James Kennedy, pastor of Coral Ridge Presbyterian Church, in Ft. Lauderdale, Florida, seldom gave an invitation for the unsaved to come forward, nor did he arrange the church service for seekers. The church service was a traditional liturgical service with stained-glass windows, deep organ tones and meditation worship, the kind that Hybels said would turn off the seeker generation. Yet, Kennedy began Evangelism Explosion, a soul-winning program that is perhaps the largest evangelistic program in the world (the leaders say that it's in every civilized nation in the world).[3]

These examples show that churches focused on evangelism don't all look the same on Sunday morning, nor does the music sound the same, nor are their sermons pitched in the same way, i.e., to win the unsaved to Christ. What is the same? Their focus, their passion and the attitude they value: they all take the Great Commission seriously.

Thom Rainer, president of LifeWay, the organization that used to be called the Southern Baptist Sunday School Board, is known for his observation on evangelistic churches that came out of his research.[4] He writes, "So how do we determine if a church is evangelistically healthy? One way is to look at a church's conversion ratio—the number of people in the church that it takes to win one person to Christ in a given year."[5]

When Rainer explains his evangelistic ratio, he says, "If a church has a conversion ratio of 3:1, then it takes three people within that church one year to win one person to Christ. While it's obviously not an exact science, our research team has concluded that evangelistically healthy churches maintain an annual ratio of at least 20:1."[6]

What we can conclude from Rainer is that "of the estimated 400,000 U.S. churches, only 3.5 percent of churches are effective evangelistically, meaning that fewer than 4 churches out of 100 maintain a conversion ratio of 20:1 or better."[7]

The Gospel Invitation

The use of the gospel invitation at the end of a service was not used throughout history, like it has been in the past 200 years. If anything, many evangelistic churches consider the invitation an irreducible minimum for soul-winning activity.

The oldest known use of the invitation was probably by evangelist Charles Finney when the Third Presbyterian Church in Rochester, New York, invited him to preach a series of meetings in 1830. The Second Great Awakening still had its influence on churches, and as Finney was preaching, people would fall to their knees and cry out for salvation, many times interrupting his sermon.

Finney was a lawyer before his conversion, and he wanted to present his "case" to the congregation like a lawyer trying to persuade a jury. Finney instructed the ushers to "usher out" those who disrupted his sermon to a private room where they could pray. But he had an alternative. The backs of the first few pews were removed to form a bench. They came to be known as "mourner's benches." After his sermons, Finney invited people to come, weep and "mourn" for salvation on these benches. Many would pray through the night.

Later, he went to a different Presbyterian church in a different New York town, and the church officials wouldn't let the backs of the pews be removed, so Finney placed chairs at the front of the auditorium for people to seek God. These became known as "anxious seats." Those who were anxious for their souls were invited to come forward after the sermon to seek salvation.

When Finney preached at a church where the church members came to the altar to receive communion—instead of taking communion in the pews—the invitation was called the "altar call." He invited people to come forward to pray for salvation at the church altar. There the invitation to be saved was given.

So while the gospel invitation had been considered the benchmark symbol of an evangelistic church, today many of the emerging churches, the praise-worship churches, and the seeker churches are doing evangelism without an invitation.

Wrap Up

There have been a number of churches that use the gospel invitation, and many still do, while many do not. It's not the invitation that's important; it's the people who come to Christ because the gospel is preached. That's imperative!

There are an abundance of churches that have never given an invitation, but each year some people come to Christ, and their lives are transformed. Beyond churches, think of those won to Christ by the Gideons, Campus Crusade for Christ, Young Life, Full Gospel Business Men's Association, prison chaplains, chaplains in the military, and so on.

When people get saved because of a church's intentional activity—or through secondary means when a member wins someone to Christ through an interdenominational agency—it demonstrates what's right with the church.

What's right with the church? Evangelism is what's right!

4

WHEN THE CHURCH IS RIGHT ON SIN

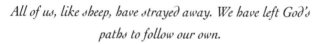

*All of us, like sheep, have strayed away. We have left God's
paths to follow our own.*

ISAIAH 53:6, *NLT*

Sin is any want of conformity into, or transgression of, the Law of God.

WESTMINSTER SHORTER CATECHISM

*Love to God is the essence of all virtue. The opposite of this — the choice
of self as the supreme end — must therefore be the essence of sin.*

AUGUSTUS HOPKINS STRONG

Sin is the one problem that keeps people out of heaven and destroys peace and happiness in this life. The church is right when it correctly understands and offers God's forgiveness of sin, and when it correctly motivates its people to live above their sin.

In an earlier chapter, I told how I began cursing as a young boy, and on several occasions tried to break my bad habit but couldn't, until I was converted. However, there were two other bad habits that I never acquired because of my Sunday School teacher, Jimmy Breland.

I was about nine years old when I was standing in front of Eastern Heights Presbyterian Church in Savannah, Georgia, between Sunday School and church. I was with four or five boys who were listening to Jimmy, our Sunday School teacher, make casual conversation when he pointed out a man tapping a cigarette on a package of Lucky Strikes. "It's something a person does right before smoking," Jimmy said. "Boys, don't ever smoke your first cigarette."

"Why?" I asked the innocent question.

It's significant to me that Jimmy didn't preach against smoking, didn't tell me it was sin or any other thing. Jimmy simply said, "You'll waste a lot of money."

It was 1940, and America was just coming out of the Great Depression when families didn't have money, and my family was especially poor. To answer my question, Jimmy Breland asked another question, "Elmer, do you like to burn up money?" Obviously, my answer was no. Jimmy said, "If you're going to smoke, you might as well take a dollar bill, gather some grass (in those days, marijuana was not called grass; he meant grass as a substitute for tobacco) and roll your own in a dollar bill." (Many poor rolled their own cigarettes to save money.)

"Don't ever have your first cigarette," Jimmy said to us. Then, in a procedure that was familiar to me from his class, he said to all the boys, "Raise your right hand and repeat after me: I promise that I will never smoke cigarettes or cigars, so help me God." We all repeated the statement after him.

Jimmy Breland was an effective teacher concerning bad habits. He strongly emphasized memorizing the Bible, so we memorized any list in the Bible, such as the 12 disciples, the 12 sons of Jacob, the 6 days of creation, the Ten Commandments, and so on. We always memorized the Bible verse of the week. Next, Jimmy told many stories to stir our emotions. Finally, he made us pledge with uplifted hand to commit our will to what we had heard. He knew that knowledge alone didn't change a life, and stirring up the emotions with stories was not enough; so he made us pledge our will with the promise of a hand.

As a result of this experience, I never smoked my first cigarette, even though my mother and father smoked. Mother came from a family of 11 children, and my father from a family of 9. All my uncles on both sides of my family smoked, but I never did, because I promised not to.

The very next Sunday, four or five boys were once again talking to Jimmy Breland between Sunday School and church. He pointed to two men and said, "Those men drink liquor; we won't let them be an elder in the church."

I took in what Jimmy said, but I knew that my father was a heavy alcohol drinker; so did Jimmy Breland. Jimmy looked us in the eyes and said, "Boys, never have your first beer." He knew that beer drinking led to hard liquor drinking.

"Why?"

"You'll waste a lot of money" was Jimmy's simple answer to us. "You might as well take that bottle of beer and pour it straight into the toilet and flush it away" was Jimmy's rationale. Then he looked me straight in the eye, knowing my father drank, and said, "Elmer, do you like to pour money in the toilet?"

"No, sir."

"Boys, put your hands up." We knew what was coming. So he said, "Repeat after me: I promise . . . I will never drink . . . my first bottle of beer . . . so help me God."

A Long Struggle

What's right with the church? It's right when it keeps young people from addictive habits that could ruin their health and even their physical life. Addictive sins can keep people from God.

America has had a long history with the struggle against the manufacturing and drinking of alcoholic beverages. In the early 1900s, evangelist Billy Sunday held crusades all over America. Not only was he responsible for more than a million decisions for Christ, but he also led a national political campaign to add the Eighteenth Amendment to the Constitution to prohibit the manufacture and sale of alcohol in the United States.

The fact that the amendment passed Congress in 1919, and eventually passed enough states to become law, is significant. Because of the terrible impact that alcohol had on American families, destroying lives and making addicts of many, and because of all the tax money needed to deal with the crime and problems flowing from alcohol consumption, the majority of Americans were willing to vote this country dry approximately 100 years ago.

In the early 1900s, most American church attendees equated drinking alcohol with sin; however, that would not be the majority opinion in today's world. This is a historical illustration to show the soul power of the American church. But it's not without exception that many people call the tax on alcohol and cigarettes the "sin tax."

When it comes to sin, the church has a twofold strategy. Because sin condemns a lost person to hell, the first strategy of the church is to offer people salvation from sin so they can become children of God (see chapter 3). A second strategy is to keep the damaging effect of sin away from its members. It usually does this by preaching against sin (warning) or by teaching how to have victory over sin. The church has always been concerned with both the damnation of sin and the damage that sin does to a life.

Obviously, the church has never said that good works, or keeping oneself from sin, ever saved anyone. "For by grace you have been saved through faith, and that not of yourselves; it is the gift of God, not of works, lest anyone should boast" (Eph. 2:8-9). And not everything the church calls sin is, in fact, sin. Just as obvious, not everything people outside the church call sin is, in fact, sin. So, what is sin?

Webster's Dictionary defines sin as "a transgression of a religious or moral law, especially when deliberate."[1] That means that sin is something that goes against what God has said, or breaks a standard that God has set. This broad definition will be acceptable for this chapter; however, most churches become much more exacting and complex in trying to examine and determine what is sin.

Remember, sin is not a thing (such as a cigarette or bottle of beer or a sex organ). Sin is an act and attitude or a response to God's standard. Sin always relates to a person's volition, or choice. So, cigarettes or a drink of whiskey is not sin; it's the act, attitude or reaction of the person against God's standard. Therefore, when a person harms his body knowingly, it is breaking God's expectations. For this chapter, however, we are more concerned with the reaction of sin on people and society than with its definition.

Look at the Ten Commandments. These were the standards God set for His people, and most of God's standards were expressed in a negative, i.e., what a child of God *should not* do, rather than a positive, i.e., what a child *should do*. Notice the things a Christian should not do (see Exod. 20:3-17 and Deut. 5:7-21):

- Place another god before the Lord God
- Make an idol of anything
- Use God's name as a curse word
- Forget the Sabbath day and not keep it holy
- Not honor your father and mother
- Kill another human being
- Have sex outside marriage
- Steal
- Lie
- Covet anything that belongs to another

The above list of 10 sins does not include a list of contemporary actions that are called sin by many churches; i.e., drinking alcohol, gambling, smoking, taking illegal drugs, looking at pornography, and so on. During times of revival, or when churches are spiritually strong, its members are committed to pleasing God—and keeping themselves from sin. When that happens, Christians live godly lives that are separated from sin.

What about the influence of godly living on society, on those who are not Christians? When individuals or society as a whole keep themselves separate from sin, there is a positive impact on culture.

When the church is right on the sin of stealing, America could save $20 billion worth of goods that shoplifters steal from merchants each year. There are approximately 23 million shoplifters in the U.S., and honest Americans have to pay higher prices for the "sin" of stealing.[2] This does not include home robberies, bank robberies and white-collar crimes, such as stealing from an employer. Everyone would have a higher standard of living if the church were more influential in preventing the crime of stealing.

When the church is right on the sin of murder, a tremendous amount of money is saved by each household in the U.S., according to statistics by the *Washington State Institute of Public Policy,* which states that it costs $885 per household to deal with the murder rate in our nation.[3]

When the church is right on sexual purity, American society is saved an abundance of money. When single mothers have babies outside of marriage, it costs the United States $112 billion per year.[4] Today's adulterers pay little—if anything—for their consensual sex outside marriage. New laws on sexual privacy and newly evolving cultural norms would never allow for the criminalizing of the acts of sex outside marriage. Yet their freedom costs taxpayers billions of dollars. If the government reached into the pockets of the noncustodial males who are parents to pay for the $112 billion that comes from taxpayers for the support of their children, young men would have a lot fewer cars, sports items or designer clothing.

More than 56,000 people become infected with HIV/AIDS each year. The Centers for Disease Control estimates that new infections cost the American taxpayers $56 billion in medical costs and treatment.[5] If the church could help all Americans to discipline their illicit sex life, think of the benefits to those who keep sexual intercourse within the sanctity of marriage.

When the church is right on the sin of lying, the American society becomes stronger in business, family and personal relationships; as a matter of fact, it becomes stronger in all social relationships. Lying on income tax forms costs Americans billions of dollars. This money could be used to reduce the tax load on every other American.

Some people will say the Tenth Commandment, "You will not covet," has little to do with life outside the church. But coveting is at the very core of gambling, the desire to get something for nothing. Look at what gambling costs America:

- 15 million people today display some sign of gambling addiction.
- Gambling profits in casinos are more than $30 billion, while lotteries are about $17 billion annually.

- The average debt incurred by a male pathological gambler in the U.S. is between $55,000 and $90,000 (it is $15,000 for female gamblers).
- 65 percent of pathological gamblers commit crimes to support their gambling habit.[6]

Social Sins

When I first became a Christian, I preached against cigarette smoking but didn't have a *foundational* verse, such as, "You shall not smoke." The best reason I could find for not smoking was "your body is the temple of the Holy Spirit" (1 Cor. 6:19). God wants us to have pure, clean bodies. My second reason was rather vague: smoking is a dirty practice; that is, smoke contaminates your clothing, your furniture, your car and every part of your life. My third reason had to do with health. When I began preaching, there were no scientific facts to back up that assertion.

Yet, my position that smoking was sin was a general position of most evangelical churches, but not churches in your mainline denominations. However, the first Surgeon General's Report raised a question based on its scientific research when it concluded, "Smoking may have a detrimental effect on your health." Later, the warning was changed to say "will cause." Then the Surgeon General's office said that smoking was "the leading preventable cause of disease and deaths in the United States."[7] When the church is right on the sin of smoking, it will save Americans billions of dollars that are now spent treating completely preventable diseases every year.

Look at the other social sin of drinking alcohol. Of course, many outside the church speak of drinking in moderation, and even some in the church today feel that drinking wine or other mixed drinks in moderation is acceptable. However, when the church is right on the sin of alcohol, notice how much money it saves America. Alcohol consumption costs Americans $150 billion in health care and treatment.[8] Look at the following statistics:

- Alcohol-related deaths kill someone in the United States every 22 minutes.
- There are 105,000 alcohol-related deaths annually due to alcohol-related diseases.
- Thirty-four percent of murders are alcohol related.
- Fifty percent of rapists had been drinking alcohol when they committed their crime.
- Alcoholic mothers are 3 times more likely to abuse their children; alcoholic fathers are 10 times more likely to abuse their children.
- Heavy drinking is involved in 60 percent of violent crime.[9]

Look at what alcohol costs businesses. An employee who drinks will call in sick 11 days more per year than one who does not. Twenty percent of employees have said in a survey they have been injured or had to cover for an employee or needed to work hard because of their coworkers' drinking.[10] And what does alcohol consumption do to a business?

- It increases the use of worker's compensation and also disability benefits.
- It increases accidents and damages incurred.

• It increases worker turnover and replacement costs.
• It creates friction among workers.
• It damages the company's reputation.
• It increases the company's liability.
• It leads to greater employee theft and fraud.[11]

Alcohol-related accidents are the leading cause of death among young people.[12] In addition, women who drink alcohol when pregnant run the risk of having a baby born with Fetal Alcohol Syndrome (FAS). According to the San Diego County Health Services, every baby born with FAS will cost the government $405,000 in direct special services, from birth to age 65.[13]

Again, look at the problem of illicit drug consumption, whether the drug is marijuana, cocaine, crack or other mood-altering drugs. What have illegal drugs cost Americans? The dollar figures for drug prevention by police are staggering. According to *CBS Nightly News*, there are 100,000 crack babies born per year.[14] The freedom and/or addiction of a mother will enslave the next generation. Isn't the church right for trying to prevent illegal drug abuse?

One more thing: for many years, the Roman Catholic church has said that divorce, except for the cause of adultery, is sin. Many historic Protestants have held the same view that a couple should not divorce except for the case of adultery. Then came "no-fault" divorce. Almost anybody can now get a divorce for almost any reason. When our government recognized the freedom of divorce, there were unintended consequences. Look at the cost to the taxpayer for single mothers and/or their families.

Where Can You See Sin?

There are some who teach that sin is an illusion, i.e., that there is no such thing as sin. The Christian Science church teaches that "sin denies God's sovereignty by claiming that life derives from matter."[15]

How do we know there is sin? Look at people's propensity to lie. What will happen when you leave a small child in a room and tell him not to touch the cookies on the counter? When you return, a cookie is missing (the propensity to take what you want that doesn't belong to you). When you ask the child, "Did you take a cookie?" On almost every occasion, he or she will say, "No!" (the propensity to deny accountability for personal failure).

To understand that people are born with a sin nature, look at the inherent selfishness in babies. A baby is born with its fists closed. Babies want their toys when they want them; everything in the world revolves around them. To discipline our selfish desires is an acquired trait.

To understand sin, look at how one person may harm another, whether it involves lying, passing on gossip, physical hurt or even killing another. Why is it that people get so angry they want to do anything they can to harm another person?

Let's look at sin like people who stand on the sidewalk and watch a building being constructed. Observers know what they see—a building is going up. But they cannot define all the technical aspects of what is happening in that building. We can look at sin the same way. When we see a sin in action, we don't know all the results impacting the person or persons involved in the sin, nor do we see all the roots that are spreading to other areas of a person or his culture.

The Original Source of Sin

The Bible describes the origin of this universe and the life of people on this planet. When God began to create one wave of life after another, it is said that when God saw all that He had done, "it was very good" (Gen. 1:31). Originally, God placed Adam and Eve, the first humans, in a harmonious community with nature, with man supervising a garden and having dominion over all the animals. But everything changed in one day.

Satan entered the garden and tempted man to disobey what God had said. God's command was slight and had nothing to do with the necessity of life. God said, "Of every tree of the garden you may freely eat; but of the tree of the knowledge of good and evil you shall not eat, for in the day that you eat of it you shall surely die" (Gen. 2:16-17).

Adam and Eve had the option of eating every other tree but one, and obviously the other trees could sustain life. God has always tested the obedience of His creatures, wanting them to obey Him and worship Him. God wants to be first in our life. Satan entered the garden to tempt Adam and Eve to disobey God's commandment. Satan did not appear as a sinister character, but as something with which both Adam and Eve were familiar, i.e., a serpent.

Satan spoke to Eve through the serpent, causing her to compromise her loyalty to God. He made God's demands sound extreme, and then he sought to show Eve how harmless it was to eat the fruit. He told her the fruit would make her as wise as God.

Satan began by placing doubts in the woman's mind concerning what God had said, and then he brought her to the point of outright disobedience.

Eve entertained thoughts that perhaps God was somewhat extreme, and perhaps God did not understand what was best for her. So, in a moment of weakness, she disobeyed God, and Adam followed suit, paving the way for all peoples who would follow their example. In that disobedience, all the consequences of Eve's disobedience spread to the human race.

How Is the Church Right on Sin?

The church teaches that sin has early manifestations in the life of children. Early in life a child has desires of anger, pride and selfishness—all giving evidence of an internal sin nature. David said, "I was born a sinner" (Ps. 51:5, *NLT*).

To counter the influence of sin, the church has sought to teach their children to obey God from early infancy. Parents are taught to raise children in a favorable atmosphere of love and positive support. Because children are so cute and warm, sometimes it's difficult for parents to teach children discipline and/ or obedience. However, when the church understands the nature of sin, it will teach discipline and obedience to children. The church can produce young people who live in a society where they exercise discipline and obedience to laws.

Second, the effects of sin are universally present in every single person, no matter where they choose to live, no matter where they were born. The Bible teaches, "There is no one who does not sin" (1 Kings 8:46). "For *there is* not a just man on earth who does good" (Eccles. 7:20, emphasis added).

A third aspect teaches that sin affects every part of the human nature—the physical, mental, emotional and social aspects of life. As Paul writes in Romans 3:10-18:

There is not none righteous, no, not one;
　　There is none who understands;
　　There is none who seeks after God.
They have all turned aside;
They have together become unprofitable;
　　There is none who does good, no, not one.
　　Their throat is an open tomb;
With their tongues they have practiced deceit;
　　The poison of asps is under their lips;
　　Whose mouth is full of cursing and bitterness.
Their feet are swift to shed blood;
Destruction and misery are in their ways;
And the way of peace they have not known.
　　There is no fear of God before their eyes.[16]

Wrap Up

Yes, the church preaches against sin, and many outside the church don't like its rules and standards. Yes, the church teaches its members to live righteous lives, and not to sin. And yes, many of those who call themselves Christians don't live by the standards of righteousness. There are church members who are addicted to alcohol, drugs, cigarettes, pornography, and so on. The church is not a perfect place, but the local church is a community of believers who strive to live as Christ would have them live.

In spite of its failures, when the church upholds the standards of righteousness and influences society around it, life will be better for all believers, and those who are not believers. The church may be wrong in the area that some of its members are hypocritical. But what's right with the church? Right standards!

WHEN THE CHURCH IS RIGHT IN AN ONGOING RELATIONSHIP WITH GOD

I beseech you therefore, brethren, by the mercies of God, that you present your bodies a living sacrifice, holy, acceptable to God, which is your reasonable service.

ROMANS 12:1

Being a Christian is more than just instantaneous conversion — it is a daily process whereby you grow to be more and more like Christ.

BILLY GRAHAM

*The Christian faith is meant to be lived moment by moment.
It isn't some broad, general outline — it's a long walk with a real person.
Details count: passing thoughts, small sacrifices, a few encouraging words,
little acts of kindness, brief victories over nagging sins.*

JONI EARECKSON TADA

The Christian must be "in the world, but not of the world" which means they must live a godly life separated from sin and be Christ's representatives on earth. When the church is right on godly living, they "shine as lights in a dark world" with a positive influence on society around them.

It seems that all religions claim that its followers can relate to their deity, and Christianity is no different. But the relationship between a Christian and His Lord is vastly different from the other empty religions of the world.

Look uniquely at how other religions expect their followers to relate to deity. The Muslim expects absolute obedience to Allah, even to the point of blowing himself up as a suicide bomber. But the Muslim doesn't believe that Allah has a personal relationship with him whereby he can walk with Allah, talk with him, and enjoy intimacy with him.

The Buddhist will give hours in contemplative meditation, with the view of emptying himself of the sorrows and evils of life. But does the Buddhist have personal conversations with his deity? The Hindu follower emphasizes *Dharma* (the worshiper's duty is fulfilled by observing social customs or law) resulting in mystical contemplation and ascetic practices.

But look at the Christian; he can meditate on the Scripture, not empty himself as the Buddhist, but rather fill himself with the knowledge and presence of God.

It All Began with Jesus

The night before Jesus died, when He knew He was leaving His disciples, He promised, "I shall be with you a little while longer . . .

where I am going, you cannot come" (John 13:33). Then Jesus explained to His disciples, "I will not abandon you as orphans" (John 14:18, *NLT*). Did you see the word "orphan"? An orphan doesn't have anyone to protect him, look after his needs or guide him through this life. An orphan is completely defenseless and alone. Jesus said we would not be completely alone, left to ourselves.

Jesus was promising that His followers would not be left to their own devices; in other words, they would not be abandoned. He would come to them in the storms of life to meet their needs. He would be with them personally to empower their ministry. He promised to work through them to move mountains (see Mark 11:23) and they could have an intimate relationship with Him.

Notice another promise Jesus made the night before His death: "you in Me and I in you" (John 14:20). This unique statement explains the Christian's relationship to Jesus Christ and hence their uniqueness in the world. Let's look at the second part of that verse first, "I in you." When a believer becomes a Christian, he has Christ come into his life. "Christ in you, the hope of glory" (Col. 1:27). This happens at salvation when the believer "received Him . . . to become children of God" (John 1:12).

No, the believer is not an orphan left to himself to struggle in this Christian life. Christ lives in him, giving him strength to live the Christian life. Thus, an intimate relationship between Christ and His followers is one of the unique features of Christianity. When the church is right on the indwelling Christ, it has the greatest potential power in the world.

When Christ indwells a believer, his life can be transformed with new attitudes, new directions and a new relationship to other believers and unsaved people. The indwelling Christ helps him overcome his temper, depression and even his psychological mood swings. The indwelling presence of Jesus helps the Christian overcome his personality weaknesses and gives him greater ambitions to serve the Lord.

This earthly world is filled with evil, trials and failures. Christians will face many temptations and sometimes will fall into sin (see Jas. 1:12-13). That means Christians do not live perfect lives, although they strive to live that way (see 1 John 1:8-10). But in an imperfect world, no one is perfect. Christians will constantly need to repent, confess their sins (see 1 John 1:9) and come back into fellowship with God.

Satan is alive and well in the world, and it is his desire to confuse, tempt and destroy Christians if he can. Satan loves to defeat their projects and persecute them. Remember that Jesus said, "If they persecuted Me, they will also persecute you" (John 15:20). But also remember that Jesus said, "I have overcome the world" (John 16:33; see also 1 John 5:4-5).

What promise do we have? When we serve the Lord and carry out the Great Commission, He has promised, "I am with you always, even to the end of the age" (Matt. 28:20). What happens when Christ lives in a Christian? He gives them courage to face dangers and strength to overcome trials, peace in the midst of the storms, and constant inner assurance that a Christian belongs to Him and that the Father is working all things together for His glory (see Rom. 8:28). Notice the intimacy we can have with Christ in the chorus of this hymn "In the Garden":

And He walks with me, and He talks with me,
    And He tells me I am His own,
And the joy we share as we tarry there,
    None other has ever known.

Now let's look at the first part of John 14:20, "you in Me." When Christ said, "You in Me," He was promising we would live in Him. And where is Jesus today? In heaven! We live in Christ as He lives in heaven.

Christians should be able to identify with Jesus Christ, who is heaven and seated at the right hand of God the Father. The words "in Christ" are found 172 times in Scripture.[1] That means that as Christians we have a unique life, as we are "in Christ."

In one sense, the believer can live triumphantly in this world because Christ lives experientially in us, i.e., "I in You." But there is a second non-experiential sense that gives the believer hope to keep on going. In the midst of trials and problems, God has promised the Christian the glories of the heavenlies (see Eph. 1:3,20). The believer is in Jesus Christ in heaven (he is there positionally, not experientially); that means we are as close to the Father as the Son is to the Father.

So then, the Christian is encouraged because of what he has in the heavenlies.[2] He has been made alive in Christ (see Eph. 2:5) and has been raised together and made to sit together in the heavenly places in Christ Jesus (see Eph. 2:6). Because the Christian is "in Christ," then in the "ages to come," He (God) will show him the exceeding riches of His grace in His kindness to us in Christ Jesus (see Eph. 2:7).

Even though Christians are not perfect in this world, yet "in Christ" they stand perfect before the Father's throne. They have the righteousness of Christ (see 2 Cor. 5:21) and they have this wonderful position "in Christ" so that they now enjoy all the riches of the Father in heaven.

Prayer Relationship

When the church is right on prayer, the church has great potential power. Obviously, all religions believe in prayer. But not all religions have the advantage of Christian prayer.

Before Jesus returned to heaven, He told His disciples, "You haven't done this before. Ask, using my name, and you will receive, and you will have abundant joy" (John 16:24, *NLT*). He was promising them that they could have a prayer relationship with the Father by praying in His name. He explained this in another place, "You can go directly to the Father and ask him, and he will grant your request because you use my name" (John 16:23, *NLT*).

Jesus expected His followers to talk with Him continually: "Men always ought to pray and not lose heart" (Luke 18:1). The Greek word here for prayer is *proseuchamai,* which comes from two words. The first, *pros,* means toward, and *euchamai* means the face. Therefore Jesus expected a face-to-face prayer relationship with His followers after He went to heaven.

Of all the words used for prayer in the New Testament, *proseuchamai* is used more than any other, suggesting that we can have intimate conversations—face to face—with Him because He lives in us. But remember, prayer is not just asking for things; rather, prayer is relationship with God where we can enjoy intimate conversations with Him.

There are many reasons for which Christians can pray. They can intercede for others (see James 5:16); they can intercede for His leaders (see 1 Tim. 2:1-2); and they can bring their needs before the Father. Don't forget meditative prayer; warfare prayer (prayer against spiritual enemies); repentance prayer after sinning; blessing others through prayer; the prayer of faith for physical healing; and another whole area of worship that involves praise, adoration, magnifying and lifting up the Lord.

Worship

Worship is perhaps the most intimate of all ongoing relationships with God. Because "the Father is looking for anyone who will worship him" (John 4:23, *NLT*), intimate worship means something to God. So ask yourself, *What did God get out of my last prayer?*

Why is the Father looking for worship? Because worship is the one thing that God cannot do for Himself. God won't worship Himself, but He's looking for meaningful adoration that comes from the hearts of those who appreciate Him and exalt Him in their lives. Jesus finished the conversation with the woman at the well by saying, "Those who worship Him must worship in spirit and truth" (John 4:24). To worship Him in *spirit* is with all of our heart's passion; to worship Him in *truth* is to worship according to the Word of God.

Revival

When the church is right on revival, it is an awesome place to be. There have been certain times in the life of the church when God "poured out [His] Spirit on all flesh" (Joel 2:28). These are

83

called by the American audience *revivals,* while throughout history and outside the United States they are called *awakenings.* This means the church of Jesus Christ has been revived from sleep, or has been awakened.

Another definition of revival is found in Acts 3:19, "So that times of refreshing may come from the presence of the Lord."

A revival is not a normal experience; it's abnormal because the church of Jesus Christ is asleep or dead. God revives His church like a person is revived from sleep or after having fainted; we speak of someone being resuscitated and revived after he has almost drowned.

In October of 1973, Liberty Baptist College was a young institution, being in its third year. The evening prayer meeting at Thomas Road Baptist Church had been over for about an hour, and students from the University were milling around in the sanctuary because the college had no campus, so the students used the sanctuary as their place to hang out or study. It was late—10:30 P.M. on a Wednesday evening—so the people of the church had gone and there was a low chatter throughout the room with students talking among themselves.

A lone student rose, walked to the pulpit weeping and began confessing his sins. The microphone and pulpit lights were off, but God was present. The student passionately repented of his sins, capturing the attention of those who were still in the auditorium. The student went down to the pulpit stairs and began praying. Several joined him to pray with him. Other students formed prayer groups around the auditorium, interceding for him.

Within a few minutes, a second student came to the platform. "You all know me; you think I'm a Christian, but I'm really not . . ." He confessed his sins and went to the other side of the pulpit to also pray on the stairs. Some other students joined him. Next, there was a young lady who said the same thing: "You think I'm a Christian, but I am not."

Sobbing and prayers could be heard throughout the auditorium. Then someone began to sing, and others joined in. Someone ran to the piano to play—softly—so as not to interrupt the sacred sound of tears. God was present; everyone could feel the atmospheric presence of God, just as they feel moisture in the sky on a cloudy day when it's not raining.

Within the hour, both the piano and organ were being played as students prayed, sang, meditated, waited on the presence of God. Because something unusual was happening, students came from their dorm rooms to join them in prayer. Church members began coming back to the sanctuary, drawn by some invisible hand or unheard voice. Around midnight, someone ran to phone Jerry Falwell. "You'd better come back to the sanctuary, 'revival's hit the church.'"

Church members awakened in the middle of the night, dressed hurriedly and drove through the dark streets of Lynchburg. All came to the church building expecting to experience the presence of God—no neckties, no Sunday dresses, each believer eager for a divine touch by God. Soon the glory of the Lord flooded the church auditorium.[3]

Some people stayed in the church auditorium from Wednesday night to Saturday morning around 9:00 A.M. All normal activities in their lives shut down. Classes were cancelled. Many didn't go to work; many fasted, not eating so they could feast on the Bread of Heaven. When drowsiness could not be fought off, students slept in the pews or under the pews or in the back foyer hallway. No one wanted to leave the sanctuary, because if they left the building, they felt they were leaving the tangible presence of God. They didn't want to miss anything that God was doing.

It was not a revival of preaching; it was a revival of testimonies and singing. Students would line up to the left of the pulpit to confess their sins or wait their turn to tell what God was doing in their life, or to share a prayer request or to ask for the singing of a song. From time to time, Jerry Falwell interrupted the procedures to make an announcement or give directions, but he didn't technically preach during the three-day revival. No one did.

Like the tide that ebbs and flows, the intensity of this experience came in waves. At times there were loud shouts of "Amen" and "Hallelujah!" as people turned to God and publicly confessed their sins. Then there were quieter times of soft weeping and private prayer around the altar.

How did the revival end? Around 7:00 A.M., Saturday morning, one student arose to confess his sins but he seemed to be bragging about his sexual conquests and other things he had done. There seemed to be no shame, no brokenness, no repentance. The Holy Spirit—who knows all about us—departed the meeting. Within an hour, everyone knew the revival was over, they left, went home or went back to their daily activities.

Doug Porter, pastor of Napanee Baptist Church in Napanee, Ontario, and I wrote a book *The Ten Greatest Revivals Ever*, where we described what God did in 10 great epochs throughout the history of Christianity.[4] After we did the research and found the great revivals, we didn't feel humanly adequate to place them in a sanctified order. We sent our findings to 17 church leaders, asking them to rank the 10 greatest revivals ever.[5] Here they are:

1. **The 1904 Revival, beginning in Wales**
   It spread around the world primarily to Korea, the Manchurian Revival and Azusa Street in the Greater Los Angeles area.

2. **The First Great Awakening, 1727-1750**
   It began with Count Zinzendorf in Herrnhut, Austria, John Wesley and George Whitefield in England and Jonathan Edwards in America.

3. **The Second Great Awakening, 1780-1810**
   It began with the Cane Ridge Revival in Kentucky and spread to colleges in America and England.

4. **The General Awakening, 1830-1840**
   The great revival of Charles Finney in New York, plus the revival in Hawaii and Jamaica.

5. **The Layman's Prayer Revival, 1857-1861**
   The revival in the Fulton Street Church of New York City, led by Jeremiah Lanphier, Dwight L. Moody and Phoebe Palmer.

6. **The World War II Revival, 1935-1950**
   The great revivals of Billy Graham and Duncan Campbell, and the awakening in New Zealand.

7. **The Baby Boomer Revival, 1965–1971**
   The Jesus People, The Prairie Revival of Canada and the Independent Baptist revival in the United States.

8. **The Pre-Reformation Revival, 1300–1500**
   The Lollards, Wycliffe, Hus and Savonarola.

9. **The Protestant Reformation, 1519**
   Martin Luther, John Calvin, Zwingli and Knox.

10. **Pentecost: The Beginning of Revival, A.D. 30**
    Peter, Ephesus and Paul.

Technically, the revival is the restoring of something that was asleep or dead. The Pentecost Revival (see Acts 2:1-47) might not be called a revival because it was not technically reviving the Old Testament kingdom of Israel. Rather, God began something entirely new, i.e., the New Testament church, the Body of Christ. However, the Pentecost Revival became the prototype by which all other revivals are measured and interpreted. Therefore, we listed it last, though it was first in history.

As we approach the return of the Lord, there will probably be other revivals, even as there are some outbreaks around the world today. However, most of them are not in the United States. There are great revivals happening throughout Argentina and other South American nations. The same could be said of great revivals in the African continent; huge churches are being built that defy imagination and count.

God is doing great works in the Pacific Rim in Indonesia and Korea.

I'm not of the opinion that the earth cannot have another revival because evil days upon us mark the end of time. As a matter of fact, I believe the opposite: the greatest revival since Pentecost can still sweep the earth before Jesus comes.

God can still do anything.

There is no sin so great that God's presence cannot revive His church. God's promises are still applicable: "If My people who are called by My name will humble themselves, and pray and seek My face, and turn from their wicked ways, then I will hear from heaven, and will forgive their sin and heal their land" (2 Chron. 7:14).

Wrap Up

I have a friend who pastors an Episcopal church. In the invocation at the beginning of the worship service, he challenges the people to meet God in an unusual encounter during worship. After you read this chapter, you may appreciate what he says, and perhaps you will attempt to practice what he promises.

He greets his congregation with uplifted hands and prays, "Today you can touch God . . . right here . . . right now . . . you can enter His presence and touch God."

Then my Episcopal friend smiles at the congregation and offers them the greatest hope that any pastor could promise a congregation.

"But more importantly than you touching God . . . God can touch you."

What's right with the church? When the church helps people touch God!

WHEN THE CHURCH IS RIGHT ON WORSHIP

You are worthy, O Lord,
To receive glory and honor and power;
For You created all things,
And by Your will they exist and were created.

REVELATION 4:11

The most valuable thing the Psalms do for me is to express the same
delight in God which made David dance.

C. S. LEWIS

When God's people begin to praise and worship Him using the biblical
methods He gives, the power of His presence comes among His people in
an even greater measure.

GRAHAM TRUSCOTT

God is seeking every believer to worship Him, because Jesus said, "The Father seeks worshipers." Worship is a two-way street that first gives praise to God, and second, strengthens believers as they give themselves in worship to God. When the church is right on worship, it is a transforming power to its members and the congregation as a whole.

Jack Hayford left the Sunday School department of the International Church of the Foursquare Gospel in 1969 to become pastor of the First Foursquare Church of Van Nuys, California, with 18 people meeting in a clapboard Army building that was transported from an Army base to the sophisticated area of Van Nuys. What was the prospect for the future?

The church had a traditional Pentecostal church service that probably didn't appeal to the people of the Hollywood film industry that populated its neighborhood. The antiquated building was adequate, but the people in the neighborhood had no time for a Pentecostal church.

Many thought Pastor Jack would use Sunday School contests to build the church, like those he promoted in the Sunday School department. But Jack had a different strategy. He said, "People will be drawn to this church by the proper worship of God, and I will build the church on worship."[1]

As a result of dynamic, life-changing worship, Hayford built a church of more than 9,000 weekly worshipers, meeting in two separate campuses each Sunday morning in four worship services.[2] He changed the focus of the people from themselves and their programs to focus on God. He changed the name to The

Church On The Way because it was located on a street named Sherman Way; also, because "the Way" was an expression from the book of Acts that accurately described the people of the New Testament who followed Jesus, who was called the Way (see John 14:6).

Pastor Jack wrote his signature book called *Worship His Majesty* to reflect his lifelong message that worship is a two-way street.[3] He called the new worship a *new* reformation or a second reformation. The first reformation came by the influence of Martin Luther who led a theology reformation in 1517. Jack wanted to introduce a reformation of methodology, i.e., a reformation of worship.

Hayford believes that many traditional churches only focus their worship on God, but when a worshiper touches God, God in return reaches out to the worshiper and transforms his or her life. Worship should be a two-way street. Hayford wanted to build a church on worship because "many will want to come— not for doctrine—but to touch God and be touched by Him."

There are many reasons why The Church On The Way grew. The church used multiple services; ministry to the poor; bilingual services; plus training its members to reach out to others, then implementing outreach programs. But the main reason the church exploded in growth was its participatory worship.

During the church's growing years, Jack wanted to break the public's fixation with traditional activities on the platform. He didn't want people to think that the sermon was the most important thing in the worship service. Neither were the special music or the choir, or anything else done by the church's leaders on the platform.

When it came time for prayer, Jack walked out into the audience to stand on a platform in the middle of the people. "Look at me, I'm standing in the midst of the people to show that God works in the midst of His people." There, Hayford explained the new focus of God working among His people. He instructed, "Divide into groups of two or three people." Then he told them to share the burden they brought to worship that morning. Next, he instructed them to pray for one another in their small group. That meant God worked through the people sitting around them; He didn't work just through the people on the platform.

Worship Plants a Church

Matt Fry was invited to candidate as pastor at a new church plant on the east side of Raleigh, North Carolina, in 1998. Matt had only been out of seminary a couple of years and was a youth pastor at Thomas Road Baptist Church in Lynchburg, Virginia.

The new church in Raleigh had adopted the name Grace Baptist Church and had approximately 25 people who came because of their Baptist heritage. A new church in a growing side of Raleigh, with a young pastor who had enthusiastic goals was a perfect match for church growth. But growth didn't come the way people expected.

Matt brought with him approximately 100 teens from his youth group; they set up a sound system, PowerPoint and a seven-piece praise band, including drums, brass and bass guitar. Matt even dressed causally (i.e., no tie). He led the people to worship God with contemporary praise worship. In his sermon, Matt explained that this was the "new method" to reach the thousands of secular people in the new communities around North Carolina's state capital. The adults were not impressed, and two leaders told him as he was leaving, "Thanks for coming, but no thanks," about being their pastor. Matt went home to forget about the experience.

That week, Matt got another phone call from the church leaders. He told them, "I thought you were not interested in me." The caller said some leaders didn't like what they heard, "But our kids loved it!" The contemporary praise worship became a part of Matt's call to pastor the church, and the church has been growing ever since.

When asked how they grew, Matt explained, "I invited public junior and senior high glee clubs or choirs to put on a concert for our church during the Sunday School hour. No school turned us down. After the concert, most of the teens, and parents who came to hear their kids, stayed for our morning service. When they heard the contemporary band and the quality of our music program, they kept coming back. We picked up three or four families after each concert."

Today the church averages more than 2,898 in Sunday worship, with a high attendance of 3,550. They recently celebrated the grand opening of their new facilities on a 47-acre piece of property.[4] The church has recently completed a building project, expanding their space from about 25,000 square feet to close to 100,000 square feet.[5] When a church does quality worship—in the music style of the people—that glorifies Christ, the people will come.

The core of worship will always be the same. Whether it is traditional worship, contemporary praise worship or a blend of the two, God will always seek worship, because Jesus said, "God is a Spirit . . . and those who worship Him must worship Him in spirit and in truth" (John 4:24, *AMP*). Therefore, when a church worships God with all its heart, that's the word "spirit"—the worshiper will be transformed. When they worship according to Scripture, that's the word "truth"—the church is doing it the way God wants worship done. When the church gets worship right, it leads to powerful influence in the believer; and through transformed people, the church influences society.

Remember: it is not how you worship; it is *who* you worship. Worship is not about you; it is about God. A lot of churches worship, but not all churches have spiritual power. Some churches are even dead in their worship service. That's because not all worship is true biblical worship, because the God of the Bible is not the object of their worship.

But there's more to worship than just the focus of the worship experience—focus on God. True worship is also measured by the response of the believer's heart to God. It is not whether you shout "amen" or you sit reverently in a pew to meditate or you "rock" to a praise band. Those who truly worship give God the "worthship" that is due Him.[6]

True worship upsets the way you live and demands more sacrifice from the worshiper. When you truly encounter God in worship, you cannot remain the same person who enters His presence. No, you must be changed when you meet God.

So that leads us to transformation, because you can't encounter the presence of God and not become better. You may repent of one previously unknown sin, or you may discover a new way to please God in your daily living; or you may completely change the direction of your life.

Worship will upset your sinful, selfish living. When you actually meet God, you can't be the same; you will change. When enough members change, then the church is changed. When enough churches are transformed, then culture is changed and eventually a nation is changed.

True worship involves change, but it also involves that which never changes. We must be careful not to get the two mixed up. First, that which never changes is God Himself. He is the object of worship; we are not the center of the church service. It does not matter if we like it or not. Worship is relationship, and that must never change. We give Him worship, and He is magnified. The question is: What does God get out of your worship?

There are the things that can be changed. Music can be played on an upright piano, a guitar, a trumpet . . . or anything that moves the heart to worship God.

The word "worship" comes from an old Scottish term "worth-ship," so the worshiper must recognize the biblical "worth" of God. We must give "worth-ship" to God in our praise, our adoration, by magnifying Him. When He is lifted up in our life, God is worshiped.

You can use soft lighting or flashing lights. You may not be able to worship in one of these choices, and the next believer may not be able to worship with your choice. Because there are so many cultures . . . because people are so different . . . because God wants all people to worship Him from their heart, worship can have different expressions, because people come from different backgrounds.

Expression of worship may differ, but relationship never changes. Ask yourself the question as you leave church next time: *Did I worship the God of the Bible sincerely, with all my heart?* Ask yourself, *Was my relationship with God deepened?*

If you didn't get anything out of worship, maybe you didn't give much, or you didn't expect much. So again ask yourself, *What did God get out of my worship today?*

The Sunday morning church service varies from street to street, and from town to town. Sometimes, you step into a sanctuary that reminds you of an eighteenth-century liturgical service located somewhere in Europe. Across the street you might enter a modern freewheeling church service that rocks. No choir, no organ, no stained-glass windows, no usual instruments of liturgy, i.e., piano and organ. And what do you see? A praise-worship team, drums, guitars, synthesizers; and they might even blow smoke on the floor. What turns you off might turn kids on to God. A teen might worship God deeper than ever before because he relates to God using the instruments of his culture.

Some people meet God in a small, humble building on dirt streets, while other people meet God in spiral cathedrals that soar among city skyscrapers, not to mention their magnificent stained-glass windows.

Some people meet God in simple do-it-yourself churches characterized by lay preaching and traditional congregational singing without instruments. Many people in the South meet God in a colonial superstructure that resembles the colonial home styles in the neighborhood, while some suburbanites meet God in mega churches that look like a civic center or a big box department store. But don't be surprised, many new churches are purchasing bankrupt big-box buildings that were previously owned by a mart but are now where the congregations meet with God; and what's cool—the building comes supplied with a paved parking lot.

Other churches don't even have a building but meet in different venues throughout the town. In *koinonia,* small-group cells meet God in living rooms, laundry rooms, weight rooms and restaurants.

Worship intensity varies from apathy in some traditional mainline denominational churches to revivalist fervor in storefront churches where people sit in folding chairs on a concrete floor and listen to a hot, sweaty preacher pound the pulpit, wave his Bible and shout at the top of his voice.

The softly lit liturgical cathedral with its deep organ tones demands reverence, while Quakers sit in silence in a plain white building with glass windows where worshipers bow in silent meditation. Pentecostal worship is interrupted intermittently with the sound of unknown tongues and shouts of "Hallelujah!" Those in Eastern Orthodox churches enjoy the mystery of symbolism embossed in icons etched in the stained glass of its windows, or cloth banners hanging from the ceiling. And in suburbia, upper-class business people worship God intellectually as they write notes from the sermon as the pastor explains the message from the original language.

What do we say about all these types of worship? The only thing that we know for sure is that churches are different from one another.

What goes on in American churches? Some churches appeal to the New England Puritan tradition: a few hymns, a couple of prayers and finally a sermon. Other churches feel like a group dynamic therapy session where the minister is the psychiatrist, helping people solve their problems from the Bible.

In a new multisite church, members enjoy Starbucks coffee and Krispy Kreme doughnuts at a round table, and then listen to a practical sermon delivered on a gigantic screen by the "communication pastor" who is located miles away at the original location. These are called video-venue churches. In African-American churches the choir sways as it sings and the pastor eloquently tells the stories of Scripture while dabbing his forehead with a crumpled white hanky. Miles away, in another church, the sermon sounds like a political rally demanding its listeners to march, rally and picket.

And what can we say about these churches? The American church has a vast number of social and cultural expressions. Just when you think you know what the American church is, you discover another expression that throws you for a loop.

What is the theology of these churches? In some Lutheran churches the congregation affirms the Apostles' Creed by repeating rote phrases that many do not understand. In reformed churches they read the Nicene Creed, then in sermonesque style the pastor explains what each phrase means. Many modern praise-worship churches have no theology; they are committed to practical Christian living and they look for sermons that will help them raise their children, become a better employee and deal with the accompanying stresses of life.

Another church believes in the theology of elegance and yet another church practices the theology of the narrative—

never going deeper than the Bible stories, like the one of David defeating Goliath, or a boy's lunch that fed 5,000 hungry listeners, or shepherds coming to worship the baby Jesus.

Still other churches swear by the footnotes of their reference Bible, which dictate what their head believes, while the sermons or the worship focus on theology.

Worshipers Are Consumers

American worshipers are consumers, and their church bulletins are menus. The type of worship is similar to the main entrée at the restaurant. Just as consumers visit where the menu fits their taste, so Americans choose a church on their comfort level. Just as Americans can pick from an abundance of options: Chinese, Mexican, fried chicken, pizza, hamburger or *bon appétit* steak; just so, the worship menus are filled with a variety of worship options.

Historically, Americans choose their church on the basis of denomination, doctrine and their family traditional background. But no longer. Now their choice is based on worship style, and they ask the question: "Will it meet my needs?" and "Will I like it?"

Worship has become like a car to get where we want to go. But worship is more than basic transportation; it has to make us feel good or feel special or fulfill our perceived image as it gets us to our destination.

America has a choice of many kinds of transportation, each one appealing to a different taste in the buyer. You can get a simple church like a small auto called a "bug" or Chevy if you have a small pocketbook and your taste is simple. You can choose a sophisticated church, like making an eloquent statement with a Mercedes. Some need a pickup truck for their vocation or lifestyle; they are like those who go to a church that offers "practical sermons" that fit their lifestyle. Others need a van or large SUV for their family, so they choose a family church with lots of activities for their kids. And don't forget the teens that would choose a church like they choose a Jeep to appeal to the "fun" side of their personality.

Liberty University graduates have planted approximately 2,000 churches, according to an earlier poll. When the University first began, most of the students planted churches like Jerry Falwell, the Chancellor of the ministry, who went door to door to get people to his church. Within 10 years, students began using Sunday School buses to bring visitors to their new church. But by 1980, the Sunday School bus method didn't work as well as in the past, or didn't work at all.

Around 1990, something changed. The old methods didn't work as they had in the past. People wouldn't let their children ride a church bus with strangers; as a matter of fact, many didn't trust a church as they had earlier in American history. And with both mother and father working, door-to-door evangelism was no longer effective. Old methods didn't work, so we had to find new methods without changing the truth of the gospel or the principle of Scripture.

Methods are many,
　　Principles are few;
Methods may change,
　　But principles never do.[7]

Today, Liberty students plant churches primarily through two organizations: (1) Liberty Baptist Fellowship, to plant independent churches, and (2) the Southern Baptist Convention, to begin a SBCV church.[8] But no matter what organization they use, I don't know of a single successful church plant that's not using contemporary praise-worship.

Six Different Worship Styles

Six distinct philosophies of ministries and/or worship styles have emerged in the thinking of church authorities. The six models came from research and observation of the American church scene. At the center of each style of worship are several adhesives, or types of "glue," that hold each church worship type together. Whereas most Protestant churches will do many of the same things in worship or ministry—pray, sing, collect money, preach and so on—the order and intensity of the things they do and the value that worshipers give to them make them each distinctive. Each ministry style adds a unique value to one's experience of worship, making it different and, to many, desirable.

The Evangelistic Church

The term "evangelistic" describes a style of ministry that emphasizes such activities as soul-winning evangelism, evangelistic preaching and the altar call. These ministries are prized among evangelistic churches' members, and because of them, members worship God and souls are won to Christ.

One example of such a church is Bill Hybels's Willow Creek Community Church of South Barrington, Illinois. (While Hybels disagrees with my assessment of his church as an evangelistic church, I cannot place his style of church in the other categories.) Hybels calls his Sunday morning service a "seeker service," where the unsaved can feel comfortable, and where barriers to their salvation are removed and sermon topics are slanted to their everyday need or experience.

We can find evangelistic-type worship services among Presbyterian, Congregational, Pentecostal, Baptist and interdenominational churches. The doctrine of a denomination is not the determining factor that makes them evangelistic, it's the way they worship that makes the distinction.

The Evangelistic church usually (1) is action-oriented, as opposed to meditative or instructive; (2) has strong pastor leadership with the spiritual gift of evangelism; (3) has persuasive evangelistic preaching to get people converted; (4) has simplistic organization; (5) is organized to get lay people involved in outreach; and (6) is platform oriented. Usually, the success of the platform ministry of preaching, special music and the evangelistic appeal will determine the success of the church.

The Bible Expositional Church

This church is usually noted for its use of printed sermon notes, PowerPoint presentations to guide people as they write out sermon outlines, verse-by-verse exposition of Scripture, the presence of reference Bibles such as the *Ryrie* or the *Scofield Reference Bible* and constant references in the sermon to the original languages of the Bible. The dominant spiritual gift of the pastor is teaching. At almost any given service the congregation can be seen taking notes.

This church usually appeals to the upper-middle class and will usually be found in a college or white-collar community. This type of worship crosses denominational lines and can be found in Baptist, Presbyterian, Methodist, Evangelical Free or a variety of other groups. The pastor probably learned his preaching style at Dallas Theological Seminary, Talbot Theological Seminary or some other independent seminary, usually not from a denominational seminary.

The Calvary Chapel movement is known for its verse-by-verse preaching, beginning at Genesis 1:1 and progressing through Scripture a chapter at a time to Revelation 22:21. The pastor might have learned verse-by-verse preaching from some interdenominational organization, such as the Navigators or Campus Crusade for Christ. Indeed, people worship God because of what they know or learn. It is an educational-based worship.

The Renewal Church

This church is usually described by its feeling and flow. Worshipers have freedom to lift their hands in worship or clap them in joy. They sing praise choruses, go to the altar to pray, hug one another and laugh or cry. It is camp meeting every Sunday morning. It is revival every time the people worship.

They lay hands on one another for healing, power or anointing. Most of the charismatic churches fall into this category and exercise the miraculous gift of tongues, healing, "word of knowledge," being "slain in the spirit," interpretation of tongues or other expressions of the Holy Spirit.

Not all Renewal churches are oriented to the Pentecostal or charismatic style or expression of miraculous gifts. I have talked to several Southern Baptist pastors who were being pressured by their local association because of the renewal style in their worship services. These churches were not charismatic in doctrine or Pentecostal in lifestyle. The members didn't speak in tongues or attempt to manifest any of the "sign" gifts. They were Baptist in doctrine and Southern Baptist in allegiance. Sometimes the pressure came from the fact that these churches had dropped adult Sunday School and extended the worship service from 10:00 A.M. to noon. The pastors told me they had not changed their doctrine; they were Baptists who supported the Cooperative Program, but their worship style was the issue.

Renewal churches can be found among Presbyterian, Episcopal, Roman Catholic, Pentecostal and the rapidly emerging independent churches. Theology is not the dividing line; hence, doctrine is not the glue that holds them together. They may preach "power theology," "prosperity theology," Pentecostalism or, in some cases, old-fashioned liberalism. However, most of them are evangelical in doctrine.

The emphasis in these churches is on personal renewal in fellowship with God. This style of worship is not found in the formal services of a liturgical church, but in the intense experience of pouring out personal love for God.

Whereas formal liturgy emphasizes one-way worship toward God (i.e., giving worship to God that is due Him), worship in a Renewal church focuses on two-way communication between the person and God. Worshipers must get something out of worship. It must be stimulating, uplifting and exhilarating. They like worship, and it affirms them. When they go home, they feel good about what they have done.

The Body Life Church

The glue that holds this type of church together is the relationships that are formed in the small groups, or cells, that make up the Body. The life of this type of church is formed in the small groups where pastoral care happens and people grow spiritually.

The Body Life church has a lot of hugging going on and places value on transparency: being open and honest and caring in their groups. They confess faults to one another, are accountable to one another and pray for one another. In some Body Life churches, this is where the offering is collected.

Body Life churches do the other things that normal churches do, such as preach, sing, teach and worship God. But they prize highly the quality of life they receive from relationships. In a given session they might testify, share burdens, pray for a hurting brother and share a blessing or an answer to prayer. It is "the Body ministering to the Body."

The Body Life church is not a pulpit-dominated church where everyone looks to the pastor for ministry. Instead, a Body Life church congregation looks to one another for support, help and ministry. It focuses on *koinonia,* or fellowship within the body.

Just as in the other cases, Body Life churches are found in Baptist, Evangelical Free, Independent or Pentecostal churches. The influence of *koinonia* crosses denominational lines. It is not a church style that is taught in most seminaries, however. Pastors learn about it from one another, from conferences, from seminars or as they intern under a Body Life church pastor.

The Liturgical Church

In some churches, this style of worship has not changed since the denomination's founding, and people sing the hymns that were sung by their grandparents. They feel that worship is transcultural and transtemporal. While some feel that a liturgical service is dead, others feel invigorated because they know they are obeying God who "is seeking such to worship Him" (John 4:23).

A Liturgical church most likely calls their place of meeting a sanctuary, meaning a place where God dwells; whereas traditionally nonliturgical churches call it a meeting house, or auditorium; or today they might call it a worship center.

They begin their service with an Invocation, to invite God's presence to come receive their worship. They probably sing the Doxology and Gloria Patri. They would not sing choruses or gospel songs, but rather, they sing hymns that focus on God. And because their hymns are prayers, they end in "amen."

Many Liturgical churches have a split chancel—one side pulpit for the preaching and another side pulpit for announcements and special music. The center of the sanctuary is the communion table, symbolic of being the center of worship. Preaching is off to the side in a secondary position.

The name "liturgy" comes from the Greek word *leitourgeo*, which originally meant "to serve" or "to minister to." The Early Church at Antioch "ministered to the Lord" (Acts 13:2). How do you minister to God? You serve Him in worship. That is why a Liturgical church will say, "Let's minister to God with the offering," which means, "We worship the Lord by giving Him our money."

Liturgical worshipers do not worship for a feeling. They center all glory, praise and worship on God. He is the focus of the worship service. The people are not there to evangelize, to listen to a verse-by-verse exposition, to fellowship or to be renewed. They worship in obedience to God.

Liturgical churches are usually Episcopal (Anglican), Presbyterian, Methodist, United Church of Christ, Greek Orthodox or those considered "high church."

The Congregational Church of the People

The Congregational church is a church of the people by the people and for the people. It is law-owned and lay-driven.

The people of a Congregational church want preaching that speaks to their hearts. They want sermons that are devotional and motivational, yet also include some teaching, renewal and worship. The pastor is a shepherd who is one of them and has arisen from them. It is a "low church," in that authority is with the people, rather than being a "high church," where authority is situated at denominational headquarters away from the people.

A Congregational church is where the people are more responsible for the church than the pastor or the denomination. It is a church where the people do the work of ministry in Sunday School, training programs, camps, VBS and the like. One of the main spiritual gifts of the pastor is to organize the people for ministry, rather than doing ministry for them.

This particular worship style best describes the explosive house-church movement that is occurring today in Communist China. There are an estimated 120,000,000 believers in house churches. Some authorities say there is a growing movement of house churches in the United States where people seek this simple worship expression.

The Congregational church is found among most Baptist, Brethren, Pentecostal, Mennonite, Quaker, Evangelical Free, and independent churches.

Biblical Basis

These six types of worship represent six basic functions or principles God has mandated the church to carry out. Each of the above six functions are found in Scripture; obviously, each of the six justify their existence and method of worship by pointing out the place in Scripture that verifies their existence. But also, obviously, they overlook the passages that justify the other forms of worship. By separating these six functions as dominant characteristics of a church, each model is better understood.

The Evangelistic church carries out the prescriptive mandate, "Go and make disciples of all the nations" (Matt. 28:19). The Evangelistic church also is reflected by the descriptive work of the Thessalonians: "From you sounded out the word of the Lord not only in Macedonia and Achaia, but also in every place your faith to God-ward is spread abroad" (1 Thess. 1:8, *KJV*).

The Bible Expositional church fulfills the prescriptive command of Paul, "Preach the word" (2 Tim. 4:2). The Jerusalem church is described this way: "They did not cease teaching and preaching Jesus as the Christ" (Acts 5:42).

The Renewal church takes a prescriptive direction, "Tarry . . . until ye be endued with power from on high" (Luke 24:49, *KJV*). A description of their revival service is, "Times of refreshing may come from the presence of the Lord" (Acts 3:19).

The Body Life church fulfills the prescriptive command of "the body edifying itself," as Paul said: "The whole body, joined and knit together what every joint supplies, according to the effective working by which every part does its share . . . for the edifying of itself in love" (Eph. 4:16).

The Liturgical church eagerly carries out Jesus' admonition, "The Father is seeking such to worship Him" (John 4:23). The elders at Ephesus were described "as they ministered [*leitourgikus*; i.e., give worship to God] to the Lord" (Acts 13:2).

The Congregational church is the prescriptive ministry of God's people, "As my Father hath sent me, even so send I you" (John 20:21, *KJV*). Paul descriptively reflects this view: "Now you are the body of Christ, and members individually" (1 Cor. 12:27).

Why are there different types of worship?

First, we worship differently because of cultural differences. God made ethnic-linguistic people groups differently, and they will retain their unique language and identity. Even though each group of people joins the rest of the Body of Christ to worship God, each group will do it a little differently because true worship must come from their innermost being.

Second, we worship differently because we have different spiritual gifts. The ministry of each spiritual gift will develop a response in believers that reflects that gift. But that response will be different from others with different gifts. We are different people but united in the one Body of Christ. Our differences will contribute to the glory of God when we worship from the strength of who we are.

Third, we worship differently because we understand the commands and principles of Scripture differently and apply them differently. We must reach lost people with the gospel and build them up in their faith.[9] There is a distinction between universal principles (we must worship God) and methods (how to worship God). A proper understanding of this discipline will help you understand why people worship differently and why God accepts each person who worships God with integrity, based on biblical principles.

Wrap Up

If there are six valid worship expressions whereby each born-again believer can worship the one true God with his entire being, then there remains some work for the Body of Christ. Christians have disagreed and they have fought. They have destroyed churches, split churches and quit churches—all over worship. They have ostracized pastors, criticized pastors and fired pastors—all over worship. We all have a lot to learn.

Because worship of the Creator is the most powerful force exerted by the creature, then it is only natural that it is going to be one of the most difficult energies to harness and direct. Like the enormous danger of atomic nuclear energy, let's pray that worship can be directed for the good of mankind, not its destruction.

What's right with the church? Worship! Some see the worship experience as the greatest strength of the church, because it is the way different people express their deepest love to God. The fact that people disagree is not a weakness, nor is it a valid criticism of the critics. Because Christians express deeply their worship to God is both a strength and a beautiful thing to see.

Some critics look at Sunday morning to see bored pew-sitters or absentee worshipers or dead services. No one can deny there are superficial worship services that put people to sleep. But the critics will see what they look for and report what they previously believed. They miss the depth of worship all across America, in all types of churches, among all types of people.

The strength of Christianity is that God sovereignly predetermined many different ways to worship Him. Worship spans history and is expressed differently in each age, but the relationship of worshipers and their God remains the same. Worship crosses cultural and class barriers, yet in all churches we see different tribes, linguistic groups and people groups worshiping God in their own way.

Their worship is different in outward forms (method), but the purpose of their worship is to magnify God (an eternal principle).

What's right with the church? Worship!

When the Church Is Right as an Interactive Fellowship

So become more and more in every way like Christ who is the Head of his body, the church. Under his direction the whole body is fitted together perfectly, and each part in its own special way helps the other parts, so that the whole body is healthy and growing and full of love.

EPHESIANS 4:16, *TLB*

The first service one owes to others in the fellowship consists in listening to them. Just as love of God begins in listening to His Word, so the beginning of love for the brethren is learning to listen to them. It is God's love for us that He not only gives us His Word but lends us His ear. So it is His work that we do for our brother when we learn to listen to him.

DIETRICH BONHOEFFER

Every Christian is exhorted to become a member of the local church,
called the Body of Christ, where they each give themselves to
strengthen others, as they in turn receive the same. And as Jesus
Christ indwells every person within a local church, so they have
maturing interaction with others who are indwelt by the same Christ.
When the church gets koinonia *right, it can transform its individuals*
to become models of love and compassion to the world.

A ll Christians are members of the Body of Christ, because they were placed "in Christ" the moment they believed. What is the Body of Christ? It is the physical body of Jesus, who sits at the right hand of God the Father in heaven. Every believer was crucified with Christ, buried with Christ, made alive with Christ and was raised with Christ to sit at the right hand of God the Father.

Because every Christian is in the Body of Christ in heaven, shouldn't each one be a member of the local Body of Christ on earth? A poll by George Barna suggests that many people want to know God, and they want to be Christians; but they want to do it outside the established church. Why is that? Is it because they have a negative view of the church?[1]

No wonder, when you consider news reports such as those of Roman Catholic priests sexually molesting young boys. But don't just beat up the Catholic Church; think also of evangelical leaders who fall into sexual sins. Remember, the world, the flesh and the devil are always tempting every believer—including leaders—to abandon what is called "strait is the gate, and narrow is the way, which leadeth unto life" (Matt. 7:14, *KJV*).

The public, in general, has other problems with the church. You can find news about declining church attendance in the newspaper, and reports of TV preachers with rich, opulent lifestyles that make people not want to attend church. Some Christians have become more loyal to their longstanding church traditions than to Jesus who indwells the church.

Others are turned off because a few church leaders preach against the way some people are dressed, or they always post an invisible set of rules by which everyone is supposed to live. Those rules seem out of date and foreign to today's contemporary society. And then there are churches that are ingrown to the point that they exclude anyone who tries to break into their fellowship. "Don't some Christians dress funny? Talk funny? Act funny?" Is it because they really are funny?

And then, churches fight one another or fight within themselves. Some churches fight over versions of the Bible, worship styles, whether divorced people can be ordained or their dislike for the loud praise band in the worship service. It seems the louder the band, the louder the criticism.

Despite all of the criticism about the local church, the real issue is "the church is Christ's body" (Eph. 1:23, *TEV*). Every believer is a member of that Body, and each has a place and a function within that Body (see 1 Cor. 12); therefore, every believer has a responsibility to care for other people in Christ's Body.

Earlier in this book, it was shown that Jesus indwelt every believer (see Gal. 2:20). So when all of the believers get together in the church body, Jesus is there within the individuals. But there's a second indwelling: "Where two or three come together in my name, I am there with them" (Matt. 18:20, *TEV*). Did you see that? The second indwelling is Christ residing in the local body; that's because the church is both a body of individuals in whom Christ dwells, and an institution where Christ dwells.

Jesus said, "I will build my church; and all the powers of hell shall not prevail against it" (Matt. 16:18, *TLB*). He is picturing a victorious church, yet as you read the New Testament, you immediately find that they had problems just as the church has problems today. Ananias and Sapphira lied (see Acts 5:1-11) and Jewish believers fussed at Gentiles getting saved (see Acts 15:1). The church in Ephesus lost its first love (see Rev. 2:4); the church at Smyrna had members who were not saved (see Rev. 2:9); the church at Pergamum had a pocket of people who served Satan (see Rev. 2:13-14). The church at Thyatira had a woman named Jezebel who was teaching false teaching and heresy (see Rev. 2:20). The church at Sardis was dead (see Rev. 3:2), and the church at Laodicea compromised with the world—it was neither hot nor cold (see Rev. 3:15). Wow, those are some serious problems! So one thing you can say is that the church didn't start off absolutely pure in the New Testament, and it got progressively corrupt each year.

Actually, two things can be said of the church. They started off in the white heat of revival when the Holy Spirit came at Pentecost (see Acts 2:1-4). But also, it had those who manifested greed and lies almost from the beginning (see Acts 5:1-11).

What Should the Church Look Like?

When you see the word "church" in the New Testament, it suggests small, intimate house churches where people gathered to pray and study God's Word (see Acts 2:46, 5:42). But there were also huge gatherings on Solomon's Porch in the Temple where many people came together to worship and declare their faith (see Acts 3:11). Both of these groups were called a church of New Testament believers (see 1 Thess. 1:1; Acts 2:47, 3:11; Eph. 1:22-23). So what does the church look like today?

The problem is that most people think the church is a building with a steeple. When they see a church in a storefront, they think it's probably out of place, but one day they'll get enough money to build a real church. Yet today, you may see churches in "big boxes," like the local shopping mart, or you may see a church in a movie theatre with a video venue presentation.

Our word "church" comes from the old Gaelic *kirk*, which became the English word "church." Technically, the word "kirk" comes from the "kirk of Scotland" which is the Presbyterian Church. Churches can look like cathedrals from Europe, southern architecture copied from southern mansions, plain white buildings with transparent glass windows or like a modern museum with flying buttresses and a contemporary steeple. Some churches meet in a home, a motel or a conference room. The largest church in the world—in history—is the Full Gospel Church of Seoul, Korea, with 750,000 members that meet on Friday nights across the city of Seoul in living rooms, apartment laundry rooms, recreation rooms and restaurants.

Have you recognized the problem? The term "church" usually describes a structure of some sort. There are times when Americans describe the church as a denomination or a family of churches. The Bible, however, never refers to the church as a building or a denomination or a family of churches. The term "church" was used to describe the community of believers who meet within the presence of Jesus Christ. A church is not described by what Christians do in the building; a church is described by who they are. However, a problem quickly arose when Christians began thinking of themselves as going to church rather than being the church. So it's only natural that outsiders see church as a place rather than the life and practice of believers.

From the beginning, a church was a gathering of Christians who were committed to the purpose given to them by Jesus Christ (the Great Commission, see chapter 11). That meant going into all the world, preaching the gospel to every person, baptizing converts in the name of Jesus Christ and teaching them to obey all things that Jesus had taught them (see Matt. 28:19-20). From the very beginning, the Early Church practiced the second priority received from Jesus, i.e., the Great Commandment of loving God with all their hearts and loving one another as they loved themselves (see Matt. 22:37-38).

Why should individuals join a church today? First, they obey the command of Christ and testify to the world that they belong to Him. Second, they join a church to serve Christ in ministry. A third high priority for joining a church is because they want fellowship and/or relationship with other believers within the church. However, statistics tell us that there are 87 attendants each week in the average American church.[2] Isn't that group a little large to enjoy intimacy?

My students from a class at Trinity Evangelical Divinity School did a survey in three churches in Wheaton, Illinois, in the spring of 1967, with a sociogram instrument, and found that the average church attender knew only 59.7 people by name, title, nickname or description, whether the church had

100 attenders, 400 attenders or 1,200 attenders.[3] It's true that you can know their names, and that's a beginning. But in the average church, you sit in pews looking at the backs of people's heads. The only persons you see face to face are the preacher and the musicians. Is this the way it should be?

However, let's not be too quick to condemn a church of 87 people, or even a larger number. Even though a church is one body of 87 people, there are many smaller groups in a local church where people get to know one another. Even small churches have smaller Sunday School classes, smaller prayer groups, men's brotherhood, ladies' Bible classes and youth meetings; and don't forget about all of the informal relationships between ushers, workers, parking lot greeters and a number of other ways that people are brought together.

Small churches are called a *single-cell church*; that's a church of 87 people. A mid-sized church is called a *multi-cell church*, which means there are many small cells within the church, where people have face-to-face relationships. The large church is called a *multiple congregational church*. That means there is more than one congregation in a single church that meets in worship. But even within each of these three congregations, there are cells in which people get to know one another.

Some large churches, however, have become *platform churches*. There is nothing more there than a Christian music concert or a Christian lecture series or a form of Christian entertainment. It's like going to a Christian movie or a Christian symphony or any platform presentation that is Christian. If there are no intimate, personal relationships among believers, can their assembly be called a church?

Biggest Little Church in the World

The Full Gospel Central Church in Seoul, Korea, is big, only if you look at its sanctuary that seats 25,000 people, and its seven worship services each Sunday. Even though the church has 750,000 members, its strength is the small cells of people worshiping, learning and praying for one another in cozy living rooms all over the city of Seoul.

When I first heard of the church, it was running 75,000 people. I thought it couldn't get any larger. But Yonggi Cho set a goal of having 100,000 people, and he reached that goal. Next he set a goal of having 250,000, and I thought that was unreachable. I visited Dr. Cho in August 1978 (my wife and I celebrated our twenty-fifth wedding anniversary by taking a mission trip to Korea).

In an interview, Dr. Cho told me, "Dr. Towns, I could have never built the largest church in the world if I followed the American practice of building sanctuaries and Sunday School buildings." Then Cho asked me, "How big is UCLA—University of California Los Angeles—how many students?"

"About 100,000 students," I said. I thought it was the largest university in America, but I was not sure about my figures.

Then he asked me, "How many blocks in the city is this university?" I told him I thought it was around 15 blocks wide and perhaps 20 or 30 blocks long, but I was not sure how large.

Cho then began to tell me that if he built a church as large as UCLA, he would have to have a church building that covered almost 100 city blocks. He explained that the city of Seoul would not let him construct that many buildings, even if he had the money. Then he said, "You Americans think of buildings when you think of church, but we Orientals think like the Bible . . ."

He asked me, "What metaphor does the Bible use to explain the church?"

"A body," was my simple answer.

"Yes," Dr. Cho said, "the church is a body; so think how the body begins and you'll understand the church."

Dr. Cho held up two fingers with a very tiny opening between them, saying, "Each physical body begins as a cell. When the semen of a man touches the egg of the woman, it produces a cell so small that it can only be seen with a microscope." He adjusted his two fingers close together to show how small a cell might be seen.

"And how does this cell grow?" Dr. Cho asked me.

I was fascinated with the conversation, so I didn't answer his question.

"A cell does not grow in size," Cho said. "If a cell grows in size, it is unhealthy, it is cancerous." Then Cho began to explain, "The body grows by the division of cells. First the one cell becomes two; the two cells become four; the four cells become eight; eight cells become sixteen . . . *ad infinitum*. The secret of a local church is to build cells all over the city of Seoul, Korea. Every time a cell gets to be 10 to 15 people, I will cut it in half and make two different cells, meeting in two different living rooms or any other place in the apartment building wherever people are living."

The secret of the largest church in the world is the small cell where people fellowship, pray and study together; and if one member is sick, they pray together for that member. If one member has problems, the other members of the cell help him or her. They visit one another, pray for one another and give to one another when one has a financial need.

The wonderful thing about a cell church is the fact that there are no limitations to the cell's growth. Wherever people live, they can meet as a cell. Obviously, in a rich neighborhood, people will gather in the living room of a wealthy home. In a poor neighborhood, the people will enjoy what meager facilities are available.

Pastor Yonggi Cho began his church in 1958, with a handful of people. Six years later, he was a dynamic 26-year-old pastor on the way up. He began every Sunday with a 4:30 A.M. prayer service and finished that night past midnight. Through his indomitable work schedule, he pushed the church forward.

Cho confessed, "I carried the whole load of preaching, visiting, praying for the sick, counseling, writing books and articles, launching a radio ministry and administering everything from the janitorial service to the Sunday School and youth groups."[4]

One Sunday after preaching for the sixth time, and personally baptizing 300 people, he collapsed in the pulpit and was carried out on the stretcher. The doctors told him if he wanted to live, he would have to leave the ministry.

During his convalescence, he struggled with the question of how he could approach the work of God and have a growing ministry, without dying of a heart attack. The Holy Spirit repeatedly hammered into his mind, "The church and the home." Then he decided to turn this ministry over to faithful shepherds who would establish home groups (cells) in their neighborhoods throughout the city.

When he told his deacons that they should each establish a home group and ministry to a group within that cell, they told him that the work of the ministry was for the pastor, which is what they hired him to do. Some even suggested he resign and let someone else carry on the church.

Dr. Cho enlisted the help of his mother-in-law—a gifted Christian leader—and she helped survey the congregation and gathered about 60 of the most suitable people for the role of church-in-the-home shepherds.

He told them, "As the Lord called me and sent me to be a shepherd, so He is now sending you as shepherds into your neighborhoods."[5] Cho testified that many of the humble folks wept because their pastor had trusted them like no other pastor had ever trusted them. They were not even the elite of his church, which included a two-star general, a congressman and a vice mayor of the city; rather, they were housewives, office workers and laborers, and two-thirds of them were women. None of them were paid.

Cell by cell, city section by city section, the ministry began to grow as cells were added. Cho kept saying to himself, *The body grows by the division of cells.* He did not follow the American way of building Sunday School classes, but created cells in homes to reach people for Christ.

I visited a cell in a Burger King at a downtown Galleria of Seoul, Korea, in the winter of 2001. I had been told that a translator would be there to introduce me to the gentlemen in this cell group and to interpret for me that evening. I was not to speak, only to observe and experience what God was doing in that cell.

As I approached the Burger King, I saw seven men at a back table in an animated and lively discussion of the Word of God. Their Bibles were open, they were pointing at verses and they were talking to one another with deep conviction. They were not arguing, not debating, but were like friends trying to understand something from the Word of God. I stood for a few minutes, marveling at what I saw.

I felt as though I were seeing the ages. They were like the Brethren of the Common Life in the Dark Ages. They were like John Wesley's Methodist groups that prayed and studied the Bible together. They were like those early Southern Baptist Sunday School classes a hundred years ago, committed to reaching unsaved people, winning them to Christ and bringing them into the church.

I prayed, and then entered and said, "My name is Elmer Towns; I'm a friend of Yonggi Cho . . ." They stared at me. It's not as though they doubted the words I said; they didn't understand a word, for none could speak English. "Go ahead, please have your meeting," I said. "Just let me sit here and soak in what is happening."

That didn't work. They sat in stunned silence, not one of them making eye contact with me. I waited a minute and then said, "Go ahead, don't let me bother you; continue your discussion." Nothing happened. After about two or three minutes of awkward silence, I realized that I was stifling the meeting. I decided it was inhospitable to wait for my interpreter, so I excused myself and left.

I departed and shopped through the Galleria for about 10 minutes, then returned. I didn't see a new person in the group, so I assumed my interpreter didn't come. Even though I didn't get to experience the words of their interaction, I saw the love on their faces for one another. I felt their acceptance for one another and their protection for one another when a stranger came into the group. I was glad I had been there.

A Church Community Is a Bonding of People

The glue that holds the church together is the shared experiences of many people. And what is that shared experience? Everyone in the church has met Jesus Christ as Savior. Each person has been indwelt by Jesus Christ. That is the one experience that all of them have in common. So, a church is a bonding of believers that have all had the born-again experience.

Going beyond this born-again experience, Christians share their dreams, problems and resources, and they support others as they receive support from them. At this point, the church becomes a sharing community.

Probably the smaller the church, the easier it is for everyone to experience community. But what happens when a church takes on more and more individuals—each with different opinions? It becomes more difficult to experience community in that church.

Has America's infatuation with the mega church hurt the very nature of its becoming an interpersonal community of relationships? Unless a mega church has a multitude of smaller groups, can it really be called a church?

The common thread of understanding one another in a local church goes back to the common experience they have in knowing Jesus Christ. They have all met Jesus Christ and know Him as Savior. That means they understand both verbally and nonverbally the experience of other people. Sometimes it's hard for some Christians to verbalize that experience, yet they understand what others have experienced and they can interact with one another on this nonverbal level.

A Church Community Helps Nurture Faith

Too often we think of faith being nurtured in a classroom where the teacher presents a lesson about growing in Christ and explains the meaning of doctrine and Christian actions. The student can learn lessons of faith and even commit facts to memory so they can pass the test. But a classroom experience is not the same as one individual nurturing the faith of another individual.

"Faith" is both a noun and a verb. As a noun, faith is a statement a person believes; it's usually a doctrinal statement or a written purpose statement of a local church. Most churches have a doctrinal statement to express the sum total of what they believe. Other churches have gone so far as to write out a statement of purpose, or how they expect people to live. When a new Christian agrees with the statement of purpose, he agrees with a noun, i.e., a thing.

However, faith is also a verb. It's something that a person does; it is a person's total response to God based on what God has said and what God has promised in His Word. As such, believers have a living faith that is growing stronger in relationship to Jesus Christ.

Usually a person grows his faith as he reads the Scriptures: "Faith comes by hearing, and hearing by the word of God" (Rom. 10:17). But just reading the Word is not enough; the

Bible must influence his emotions so that he loves God and fears sin. Beyond intellect and emotion, the Bible must touch the will; a person must yield himself to God and choose to follow God's plan for his life.

Faith formation usually happens in a community where a new believer sees old believers living for Jesus Christ, serving Him and worshiping Him. The new believer assimilates these living examples of faith; hence, the church becomes a nurturing community.

So, how is faith nurtured? It usually begins when young believers get a desire to serve God. So role models are necessary in a faith-nurturing community. Then, as the new believer begins to grow into greater areas of response to God, he becomes more accountable. Thus, within the faith community, young believers discover their spiritual gifts and calling, then they begin to serve God.

The next step in faith-nurture is developing values and attitudes. These usually cannot be taught, *but must be caught*. The new believer must learn to be honest, pure and obedient to God, and be helpful and respectful toward, and pray for, other people.

A Church Community of Faith Allows for Diversity

When people become a part of a church, they usually affirm their faith in a public statement as they begin interacting with a local group of believers, each of whom are different from them. A church has a corporate group of values and attitudes, and all of those in the church will embrace those corporate values and attitudes. But at the same time, each individual has some values and attitudes that are different from those of the other people.

What are those corporate values they all agree upon? They agree on the importance of being born again, of knowing Jesus Christ and the effect of regeneration on their life. They agree upon the importance of prayer, separation from sin and the worship of God. They also agree on the necessity to support their church by prayer, tithes and ministry. And again, they agree on the necessity of the Great Commission—to reach out, with other churches, to preach the gospel around the world. They agree that Jesus Christ is coming again to receive them to heaven, so they live in light of His coming and are prepared at any moment for His return.

But people are different in their relaxation, recreation, reading habits and even the things they watch on television. They do not dress the same, eat the same food, drive the same kind of cars; nor do they work at the same type of employment. Their differences bring color and hue to the local congregation; their "common agreement" brings strength and purpose to the local congregation.

The glue of sameness is the cohesiveness they bring to the church congregation. The glue of "differences" is a manifestation of God's grace and power that gives them a heart for one another, so they can serve together even though different.

The fact that they are a faith community encourages cordiality. They must respect one another, love one another, accept one another and serve one another. Yet, they must have the freedom to give to one another and receive from one another; hence, reciprocity is necessary in a faith community.

Because the church community is held together by faith experiences, the glue is never doctrinal or a written creed or set of rules. Yes, to become a part of a community a person must subscribe to a specific doctrinal statement, but the community that Jesus established is much deeper than rules. The faith community must share Jesus Christ. Because these people have been transformed by Jesus Christ, newness of life indwells each of them, and each person gives to the others and receives from the others as Christ has given to them.

A Church Community Is a Community of Conviction

The convictions that hold our community together are much deeper than written rules, principles or even signed covenants or pledges. People are voluntarily drawn to a church community because they expect the type of life from others that they also enjoy. They are experiencing together what they would otherwise experience separately.

What do they value? First, everyone in the church community has a deep commitment to the values and attitudes of the Scriptures; and second, to the values and attitudes of the other individuals in their community. As each individual expresses his or her personal values and attitudes, and shares in the experiences of others, the church becomes stronger; it becomes a community of conviction. Each has a shared sense of how to live for God and what made their church so attractive to them in the first place.

A Church Community Is a Mentoring Agent

Most church communities have a membership class to attend before a person joins a church. Whether you call this education, indoctrination, instruction or discipling, it's a formal attempt to communicate to new members what the whole group believes. As good as this specific learning experience is, the life of the community is usually transferred to new members by nonverbal experiences.

New believers are accepted for who they are, but they soon feel pressure (realized or unrealized) to become like the others in their church. They want to live the way others are living, value the things that other people prize and get the results in prayer that others are getting. This process is usually informal.

As a result, it is usually not any one person in a local church that leads new members to accept the values and experiences of the church; it's the whole church mentoring every new believer.

This happens when the church offers a network of acceptance in which the new Christian feels recognized for who he or she is, and for what he or she is becoming. Therefore, everyday informal experiences are where the church is most powerful in its mentoring focus.

A mentoring church community does two things. First, it is the standard that challenges each new believer to enter into that life. Second, it's the supporting network of relationships that encourages people to come up to that standard.

Wrap Up

The church is not a mental health support group, but when its members fellowship with one another, it performs the function of a support group—and much more.

The church is not a therapy group that helps each member analyze his or her individual problems in a group endeavor, seeking a workable solution to a problem. But the church is a place where individuals see their problems through the eyes of other members, and in the light of God's Word, solutions are found and applied. The church is a place that helps individual members find emotional, mental and even physical therapy, but the church is not a therapy group, it is much more.

The church is not a discussion meeting to define and solve problems, but it is that and much more.

The church is not a city council that determines the practice of those who live in its community. It may be that, but it's much more.

The church is not a classroom to learn new facts and discuss new ideas; it may be that, but it's much more.

The church is not a fellowship group—like men playing golf together or women on a bowling team—where the burdens of life are forgotten and the sweet joys of laughter are enjoyed. Yes, it is a fellowship group, but it is much more.

The church offers deeper healing than any therapy the world can offer. The church has better knowledge and deeper insight than any class can ever teach. The church has access to solutions to the most intricate problems ever faced. The church provides more affirming fellowship to the hungry needs of people than found any place else.

Why?

Because the church is Jesus Christ. It is called the Body of Christ. Those in the church are joined to Him in eternal salvation, for Jesus indwells each believer individually, and He lives among the believers in the church. The church enjoys the spiritual presence of Jesus, and those in the church know something in their hearts that no one outside of Christ possesses.

What's right with the church? Interactive fellowship!

WHEN THE CHURCH IS RIGHT ON HELPING NEEDY PEOPLE

"For I was hungry and you gave Me no food; I was thirsty and you gave Me no drink; I was a stranger and you did not take Me in, naked and you did not clothe Me, sick and in prison and you did not visit Me." Then they also will answer Him, saying, "Lord, when did we see You hungry or thirsty or a stranger or naked or sick or in prison, and did not minister to You?" Then He will answer them, saying, "Assuredly, I say to you, inasmuch as you did not do it to one of the least of these, you did not do it to Me."

MATTHEW 25:42-45

Considering all the good work done by all of God's people, in all the ages . . . Jesus has caused far more people to give far more help to far more needy than any other humanitarian person in the world.

UNKNOWN

When the church gets social action right, it can impact the world with its message of redemption from sin, and become an example of Christ, who "did not come to be served, but to serve" (Mark 10:45).

The essence of Christianity has always been a focus on "others." One of the greatest Christian social movements in history has been the Salvation Army. Its leader was General William Booth, who organized the Salvation Army in the 1800s to preach the gospel among the poor of England and to minister to their daily needs. This was no normal church; he wanted his followers to be like soldiers, so he dressed them in uniforms and drew the masses to street meetings with blaring brass horns and booming drums. Here he preached the gospel, encouraged people to repent from all outward sins and to kneel and receive Christ.

The Salvation Army organized soup lines to feed the hungry, orphanages to care for homeless children, hospitals for the poor and homes for pregnant unmarried girls. As the Army grew stronger and larger over the years, it branched out into an ever-widening field of humanitarian aid.

When Booth was too old and feeble to attend the annual massive convention of the Army, the leaders asked that he write a sermon to be read to the assembly. In response, General Booth sent a telegram with one word: "Others."

Perhaps the desire to help others comes from the second half of the Great Commandment of our Lord, not the Great Commission that involves evangelism. The Great Commandment says, " 'You shall love the LORD your God with all your heart, with all your soul, and with all your mind.' This is the first and great commandment. And the second is like it: 'You shall love your neighbor as yourself'" (Matt. 22:37-39). Therefore, when a person becomes a Christian, he should first of all love God with all of his heart and immediately turn outward to others and love them as much as he would love himself. What's right with the church? The church is right when it helps others.

The Great Commandment was the topic of Jesus' interaction with the religious establishment. When one questioner tempted Jesus saying, "What shall I do to inherit eternal life?" (Luke 10:25), Jesus referred him to the Law, or the Torah, and asked the man what it said about the greatest commandment. The debater answered what was repeated earlier, "'You shall love the Lord your God with all your heart, with all your soul, with all your strength . . . and with all your mind,' and 'your neighbor as yourself'" (Luke 10:27).

Rather than telling the religious leader, "You must be born again" or to repent, Jesus pointed out that he must love his fellow man, and then told the story of the Good Samaritan. This story could have been a tinderbox for the Jews, for they had nothing to do with the Samaritans.

Jesus told His listeners that a Jewish man left Jerusalem and went down to Jericho, but fell among thieves who robbed him, mugged him and left him for dead. First a priest passed him by, then a Levite; these represented the religious leaders of Israel. They did nothing for the poor man. Then Jesus told how a Samaritan (Samaritans were despised by the Jews) bandaged up his wounds, took him to an inn, paid for his lodging and then offered to pay if there were any other expenses.

Jesus asked the question, "Who is my neighbor?" The answer is very simple; the one who is in need is our neighbor. It's not always our next-door neighbor or someone else living in our apartment building. Thus, Christianity has always been focused on needy people.

Under the preaching of John Wesley and George Whitefield, the First Great Awakening swept England in the 1700s. Most people who came to know Christ were from the poor or ignorant working classes. The movement was based on Wesley's new "methods" of evangelism. Most of Wesley's emphasis was on evangelism and discipleship.

The Methodist Church was a contradiction to the Anglican Church, which was the state church, supported financially by the crown. Every new baby born in England was baptized into the Anglican Church. Many of the Anglican churches fought John Wesley and the growth of the new Methodist church, but the Anglican Church in Clapham Crossing, a wealthy district on the southwest of London, was deeply influenced by the revival. Its pastor, John Venn, was touched spiritually by the revival, and later his preaching touched the aristocrats of his church.

William Wilberforce (1759–1833), a member of Parliament and a member of the Clapham Church, was disturbed over slave trade, especially the trafficking done in British ships. As Venn preached against slavery in his pulpit, Wilberforce preached against it in parliament, and after many years of disappointing defeats, Wilberforce got the Foreign Slave Trade Bill passed in 1806 to ban slavery from British ships. It was almost 60 years later before President Lincoln of the United States would issue the Emancipation Proclamation in 1862.

There were other members of the Clapham Church, called the Clapham sect, who turned their attention toward what is called the "social gospel" or helping needy people in their desperate conditions. Granville Sharp improved the working conditions in the city and was one of the first British campaigners for the abolition of the slave trade. He also involved himself in trying to correct other social injustices.

Anthony Ashley Cooper (later given the courtesy title of Lord Ashley) (1801–1885) and Michael Sadler campaigned against child labor, passing laws against children under the teenage years working in mines and mills. In the 1800s, Lord Ashley began to take an interest in social issues after reading reports about investigating child labor, and he became the new leader of the factory reform movement in the House of Commons. A new act proposed by the House of Commons resulted in the 1833 Factory Act passed by Parliament. Under the terms of the new act, it became illegal for children under age nine to work in textile factories, whereas children between the ages of 9 and 13 could be employed for a maximum of eight hours a day. The main disappointment of the reformers was that adolescents from 14 to 18 were allowed to work up to 12 hours a day, and factory owners would continue to employ very young children.

In 1840, Lord Ashley helped set up the Children's Employment Commission. Its first report on mines and collieries was published in 1842. The majority of people in Britain were unaware that women and children were employed as miners. Later that year, Lord Ashley piloted the Coal Mines Act through the House of Commons. As a result of this legislation, women and children were prohibited from working underground.[1]

Elizabeth Fry (1780–1845) attempted to improve the inhumane conditions of prisoners in English jails and worked for reform, including those that became themes for her: segregation of the sexes, female matrons for female prisoners, education, employment (often knitting and sewing) and religious instruction. After a number of years dealing with personal difficulties, she returned in 1816 to the prison system and began a ministry to establish a school for their children. Shortly thereafter, Elizabeth organized a group of women into the Association for the Improvement of the Female Prisoners in Newgate. This group organized a school and provided materials so the prisoners could sew, knit and make goods for sale. The group became involved in visiting the prison and reading the Bible to the prisoners.[2]

Good Works for What?

Christians know they are saved by grace through faith without good works, "For by grace you have been saved through faith, and that not of yourselves; it is a gift of God, not of works, lest anyone should boast" (Eph. 2:8-9).

But James adds a different page of requirements for Christian discipleship. He admonishes, "Has God not chosen the poor of this world to be rich in faith and heirs of the kingdom?" (Jas. 2:5). Then James turns his criticism, "But you have dishonored the poor man" (v. 6). He asks the question, "If a brother or sister is naked and destitute of daily food, and one of you says to them, 'Depart in peace, be warmed and filled,' but you do not give them the things which are needed for the body, what does it profit?" (vv. 15-16). Then James concludes, "Faith without works is dead" (v. 20).

So, what's right with the church? Her good works! Look at the number of hospitals in the United States started by Christian organizations, whether they were started by Baptists, Catholics or any other Christian organization. Hospitals began in the Eastern part of the Christian Church, inspired by Christ's example of serving and caring for the poor, the sick and the needy. They spread rapidly to the West and were closely associated with religious orders and their duty to offer hospitality to any in need.[3] Then look beyond that to the colleges, orphanages, homes for unmarried women and adoption agencies. But don't look at just the large hospitals or any other institution; look into the local church at what is being done.

Steve Sjogren began the Vineyard Community Church in Greater Cincinnati, Ohio, in 1983, and focused on meeting the needs of people. Steve had run into people who thought he was in the ministry for money, or for the glory of preaching or for any other of various reasons; but Steve took mop, bucket and cleaning supplies and began going from gas station to gas station volunteering to clean bathrooms. When he approached a surprised attendant, he asked, "Can I clean your bathroom?"

"Why . . . why would you do that?" was the normal response.

"I want to show you what my Lord Jesus would do; He would serve people and do the dirtiest of jobs."

Steve Sjogren's reputation and the reputation of his church community gained citywide recognition. One of the city parks had been taken over by gangs and was the primary place for the buying and selling of drugs. The Vineyard Church went to the park, cleaned the graffiti from the walls, refurbished the benches, put new plumbing into the bathrooms and water fountains, replanted bushes and grass and did a complete refurbishing job on the playground. When it was done, the mayor, city council and many other community leaders came for a dedication of the refurbished park, and the people found a renewed interest in their community.

Sjogren said, "We desire to show God's love in practical ways to people all over the city." This is a relationship approach to evangelism that opened up many ways for them to preach Jesus Christ. But it was more than pure evangelism; Steve said, "We believe small things done with great love will change the world."[4] As a result, the church members make a habit of performing everyday services for all types of people throughout Cincinnati.

Roscoe Lilly Failed

Roscoe Lilly graduated from Liberty University in 2008 with a Master's of Divinity degree and went to Greater Albany, New York, to start NorthStar Church in Clifton Park. He did it the way Jerry Falwell told him to do it, following saturation evangelism, i.e., "Reaching every available person through every available means."[5] But something drastic happened.

Roscoe mailed 30,000 invitations to the surrounding neighborhoods. He put flyers in 7,000 homes and made 400 front door contacts with people. No one came the first week to their rented school buildings. No one came the second week, nor did anyone come the third week or the fourth week.

Roscoe withdrew to take stock and went to Liberty University to be trained in servant evangelism. Then Roscoe and his wife began cleaning bathrooms in convenience stores and other public places to demonstrate to the people of Greater Albany what Jesus would do to get people to listen to the gospel. After five years, they had a big attendance day of 275, but Roscoe knows that both he and Jesus "did not come to be served, but to serve" (Matt. 20:28).

Thomas Road Baptist Church of Lynchburg, Virginia, determined in the fall of 2008 to do good deeds in the church. First, they began by taking dozens of Krispy Kreme doughnuts and coffee to every firehouse in Lynchburg, once a week, just to say, "We appreciate what you do for us and our city." The church targeted three city parks to completely refurbish them for needy neighborhoods. It also adopted San Leon Community Church, in San Leon, Texas, which was destroyed by Hurricane Ike. A team of 66 workers went in January 2009 and collected $50,000 to completely restore the church to its previous operating level.

At home, Thomas Road volunteers paint homes, repair porches, replace shingles and do all types of handiwork among the poor of the church or the elderly who cannot help themselves. In addition to that, an evening clinic—The Ruth Brooks Clinic—is available once a week in the downtown city section of Lynchburg, staffed by professional doctors and nurses, where free medical services are provided to the needy of the area who do not have any health care insurance or access to medicine.

Helping Alcoholics

Good works have always been in the history of Thomas Road Baptist Church. When the church was one year old, Jerry Falwell led many alcoholic men to Christ who were so addicted they couldn't break their alcoholism. A man would come forward in a church service, give his heart to Christ, but within the next two or three weeks he was back into alcohol. So, Jerry opened Elim Home in Appomattox County, where a man could come free of charge, stay for 90 days and receive spiritual support, counsel and help, all in the name of Christ.

The vision of helping the needy captured the unchurched Lynchburg community. A reporter from the local newspaper printed a feature article telling the story of how men were helped, but the home in the county had no electricity, no running water and only an outside toilet. A few days later, a helicopter landed in a pasture near the farmhouse. James Cooke, the executive director of an electrical cooperative for several counties of Virginia, followed by his key aides, came to survey that old farmhouse where Elim Home was located.

"The nearest electric line is more than one mile up the road," Cooke reported after a quick tour of Elim Home. "But I've called for a crew on my radio, and you'll have power here right away."

"But we don't have any wiring in the house," Falwell answered sheepishly, "and we don't have any money to hire somebody to wire it."

Again, Mr. Cooke had the solution. He had already called the right person for help. "I've called Dan Candler," he said. Dan Candler owned Mid-State Electric Company. "Dan will get your place wired," Mr. Cooke promised, "and will throw in a few other little things as well."

A complete wiring job was followed by truckloads of stoves, refrigerators, heaters and various appliances. Then came a plumbing supply house truck and crew to put in bathrooms; a septic company appeared to dig and install a septic tank.

The rules of Elim were (and are) simple. The men had to come voluntarily; they could not be consigned to Elim Home by a wife or by the court. Elim was not a drying-out place; they must come sober. It is a place for total deliverance. The men must sign themselves in. They must quit drinking "cold turkey," that is, without the aid of other chemicals or continued small doses of alcohol. They cannot leave in less than 60 days, and they must participate freely in the activities of the Home.

In the 50 years since Elim Home was founded, thousands of men have come—22 at a time—and they come free. About 50 percent of them never drink again. That's not a great percentage, but it's outstanding when government facilities have less than a 20 percent success rate.

What's right with the church? Delivery from addiction!

Helping Unmarried Pregnant Teen Girls

Helping alcoholics was not all that Jerry Falwell did. When he began preaching against abortion in 1979, he quoted the old motto, "It's better to light one candle than to curse the darkness." So he began Liberty Godparent Home where a young pregnant girl could receive room, board, medical treatment and delivery of her baby—all free. Then, to make sure that everyone knew the heart of the church was in the right place, both the mother who gave birth to the child and the child were given a free scholarship to Liberty University.

Between 1990 and 2002, my wife, Ruth, was the director of the Family Life Services (the adoption agency of the Godparent Home). During that time, she placed 242 babies in the arms of adoptive parents, babies who might have been aborted had not Jerry Falwell seen a vision of helping young, needy pregnant girls. What's right with the church? Saving babies.

Not Just Being a Good Neighbor

When a church reaches out to a community to do something with nothing expected in return, it's not just being a good neighbor, nor is it a pre-evangelism endeavor. They follow the example of Jesus who said, "Just as the Son of Man did not come to be served, but to serve, and to give His life a ransom for many" (Matt. 20:28, *NASB*).

Think of the time when Jesus preached to 5,000 hungry people (see John 6). He went the second mile and fed them all because they were hungry.

Think of the many times when He saw hurting people and sick people, all needing physical attention. What did He do? Jesus healed them. Following His example, the Church should pray for the sick and hurting, but it should do more than just pray. When it has medicine, it should share its medicine; when it has doctors and nurses, it should share their services. When it has beds for the sick, they should be supplied.

Good works begin with an attitude of being like Jesus. Look at the night before the Lord died. What did He do? He washed His disciples' feet. What an example of humility and servicing one another! Read what He said:

> Do you understand what I was doing? You call me "Teacher" and "Lord," and you are right, because it is true. And since I, the Lord and Teacher, have washed

your feet, you ought to wash each other's feet. I have given you an example to follow. Do as I have done to you. How true is it that a servant is not greater than the master. Nor are messengers more important than the one who sends them. You know these things—now do them! That is the path of blessing (John 13:12-17, *NLT*).

At another place, Jesus commended good works as He described the last judgment when people will give an account of themselves before God. Jesus told those gathered before Him, "For I was hungry and you gave Me food; I was thirsty and you gave Me drink; I was a stranger and you took Me in; I was naked and you clothed Me; I was sick and you visited Me; I was in prison and you came to Me" (Matt. 25:35-36).

But the people didn't understand. They replied, "Lord, when did we see You hungry and feed You, or thirsty and give You drink? When did we see You a stranger and take You in or naked and clothe You? Or when did we see You sick, or in prison, and come to You?" (vv. 37-39). "And the King will tell them, 'I assure you, when you did it to one of the least of these my brothers and sisters, you were doing it to me!' " (v. 40, *NLT*).

Wrap Up

Today we hear much about the DNA of parents affecting their children. We carry the spiritual DNA of Christ, who gave Himself for all, and served all people unselfishly. What does this mean? Because a Christian has Christ in his life—because he is born into God's family—he or she does what Christ did.

What's right with the church? Helping the needy!

WHEN THE CHURCH IS RIGHT ON THE FAMILY

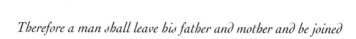

*Therefore a man shall leave his father and mother and be joined
to his wife, and they shall become one flesh.*

GENESIS 2:24

*Each day of our lives we make deposits in the
memory banks of our children.*

CHARLES R. SWINDOLL

*What should it profit a man if he gains the whole
world and loses his whole family?*

JERRY FALWELL

When the church rightly influences the family, it has a deep influence on society and the individual. Because the family is the first influence on the child who will eventually take his or her values and attitudes into the culture, and because the family has a continuing influence on individuals, the church helps to shape every area of life when it influences the family.

The family is one of the foundational units of society, and because of this, when the Church's focus is right on the family, nations are strengthened, society is reinforced and individuals become stronger.

The traditional, nuclear family (also called the biological family) is under attack to a greater degree, perhaps, than in any other time in history. These attacks come from government, media, special agenda groups and, generally, by those who reject the Ten Commandments and biblical standards that define the family.

The government helped to undermine the family by making no-fault divorce easy and by not holding absentee fathers financially responsible for the care of the child they had fathered.[1] Media has undermined the family by glorifying sex outside of marriage, which produces many problems associated with single-parent moms. Media also mocks the traditional family, all the while pushing a homosexual agenda.

Special-agenda groups file lawsuits to block laws that protect the traditional family, while supporting actions that allow individualism to trump family responsibilities.

Other factions that tear apart the traditional family are: an economy that demands that moms work; intrusive social agen-

Trend in Media/Television Portrayal of Families[2]

1950s *Father Knows Best*
       I Love Lucy
       Leave It to Beaver

1960s *The Dick van Dyke Show*
       Family Affair — single father, with butler, raising
          two kids
       The Brady Bunch — blended family

1970s *Happy Days* — focused more on kids than family
       All in the Family — highly dysfunctional family,
          i.e., Archie Bunker

1980s *The Cosby Show*
       Full House — three men raising a family together
       Kate and Allie — two divorced women raising their
          kids together

1990s *Roseanne* — dysfunctional family
       The Simpsons — mockery of family roles
       Married with Children

2000s *Two and a Half Men*
       Family Guy — prime-time cartoon dysfunctional family

cies that take children from parents who discipline them; laws that prohibit caregivers from reporting teen pregnancies to the parents; feminist groups that mock the traditional value of mothers in the home; those who promote an activist anti-family role for women.

Then there is pressure from all types of groups that react negatively to the Judeo-Christian ethics upon which this nation was founded—for example, groups that would distribute free condoms to high school students in their opposition to the Christian ethic of sexual purity; i.e., saving oneself for marriage. These and many more subtle, but dangerous, trends all erode the stability of the family, which has been the backbone of America's strength. Ellen Goodman (a liberal feminist) wrote in *The Boston Globe*:

> Americans once expected parents to raise their children in accordance with the dominant cultural messages. Today they are expected to raise their children in opposition to them. Once, the chorus of cultural values was full of ministers, teachers, neighbors, leaders. They demanded more conformity, but offered more support. Now the messengers (of a new family ethic) are violent cartoon characters, rappers and celebrities selling sneakers. Parents are considered "responsible" only if they are successful in their resistance. That's what makes child raising harder. It's not just that American families have less time with their kids; it's that we have to spend more of this time doing battle with our own culture.[3]

In this chapter, the family will be described as a group of persons related by marriage and blood ties, and generally living together in the same household. Therefore, a family is defined as "the choice of one man and one woman who bond together in a permanent family relationship."

The Biblical Basis of the Family

Before looking at how churches are trying to minister to the family and preserve family values, we must first establish the biblical basis for the family. Throughout the Bible, the family is held up as the ideal social relationship for adults and children even though there were many violations of this rule. Even in the Bible, individuals violated the social network of the family and refused to follow God's pattern. The Bible describes adultery, sex among singles, polygamy, keeping concubines and homosexuality, all the while not approving of these actions. Individuals violated the social network of the family either for lust, convenience or for whatever reason. When they did, the Bible shows disapproval and records the problems of those individuals who rejected a monogamous, heterosexual family relationship (see Deut. 6:6-25; Eph. 5:21-6:4).

Abraham experienced negative consequences by having sex with a concubine, Hagar. Jacob had two quarreling wives. David had more than one wife and Solomon had 700 wives and 300 concubines. It destroyed him spiritually: "He had seven hundred wives, and three hundred concubines; and sure enough, they turned his heart away from the Lord . . . they encouraged him to worship their gods" (1 Kings 11:3-4, *TLB*).

God Planned the Family from the Beginning

From the very beginning God planned for the family by creating a man and woman: "God created man in His own image;

in the image of God He created him; male and female He created them" (Gen. 1:27). So from the beginning God created two individuals differently, but at the same time He planned to join them together.[4]

One of the first tasks in the Garden of Eden was for Adam to name the animals (see Gen. 2:19). But in response to this task, Adam realized there was no female for him: "But for Adam there was not found a helper comparable to him" (Gen. 2:20). If Adam wondered about a companion, quickly God remedied the situation.

God put Adam to sleep and took one of his ribs to fashion a woman. What did God do then? He performed the first marriage ceremony. How did the man respond? "And Adam said: 'This is now bone of my bones and flesh of my flesh; She shall be called Woman, because she was taken out of Man.' Therefore a man shall leave his father and mother and be joined to his wife, and they shall become one flesh" (Gen. 2:23-24).

The creation of the first family made such a great and indelible influence that when Jesus taught the multitudes, He quickly reinforced God's original plan for marriage by adding its ethical requirements: "They are no longer two but one flesh" (Matt. 19:6).

As a result, Eve, the first woman, is the "mother of all living" (Gen. 3:20). Therefore, from Adam and Eve came the first children. She was as much a rational and accountable person as was Adam, and because of that, she shares equally with Adam as the source of the human race.

When Adam and Eve fell into sin, different divine consequences fell on the woman than on the man. Eve would have pain in childbearing (see Gen. 3:16), and Adam would have pain in work (see Gen. 3:17-18). It seems Eve would bear the children in pain but enjoy the rich benefits of rearing them. Adam was to provide the economic resources for the family.

It seems that the monogamous family survives several generations after Adam and Eve left the Garden until Lamech was described as having "two wives" (see Gen. 4:19-24). The record of Genesis 4 shows that man forgot his original relationship to God and was guilty of all types of devious acts in social and personal rebellion against God. Lamech was the first to break the monogamous family, and he became a murderer and confessed, "I have killed a man for wounding me, even a young man for hurting me" (Gen. 4:23).

The Ten Commandments

When God set up the Ten Commandments, they were foundational to the monogamous family. The first four commandments pertain to our relationship to God. Commandments six through ten relate to social relationships, and of these, the fifth, seventh, and tenth commandments point to the monogamous family.

The fifth commandment says, "Honor your father and your mother" (Exod. 20:12). This refers to the relationship of children to parents in the family unit. The equality of father and mother is stamped into this commandment. Mother is honored as a head of the family as well as the father. Thus, there is no question as to her position of honor and authority in this commandment. Therefore, in God's eternal plan, the woman was never chattel, property or an inferior being, but she was a mother, her highest calling in life. The mother is not subordinate but equal with the father in receiving reverence from the children.

No matter how people try to reinvent history, this biblical reference to a mother could not be true if she were a member of a harem or one of two or three wives in the family. God's plan was always a "one woman and one man" family, even when there are incidences of men in the Bible with more than one wife or concubine; i.e., Abraham, Jacob, David, Solomon.

The seventh commandment again raises a strong wall of defense for the family, "You shall not commit adultery" (Exod. 20:14). In this case, adultery and fornication are synonymous. God says it is unlawful to have sex, whether one or both of the parties are married or not. All and any sex outside of marriage is barred by this great family ideal. Therefore, to God, all sex outside sex with one marriage partner is sin.[5]

A society where man runs around fulfilling his sexual needs by seducing every sexual partner he can find is contrary to God's standards and will ultimately undermine society's strength and perpetuity. Thus, as America moves further away from Christian ideals, sex outside of marriage has become more and more prominent, and erodes the moral fiber of the nation.

Also, where motherhood is reduced to simple childcare during the short period of childhood, and she must work to support herself and children, she should receive parental support from an absent father. But the inability of the government to enforce this principle also contributes to the erosion of the moral fiber of the family and also the nation.

The tenth commandment again speaks to a strong marriage, "You shall not covet your neighbor's house; you shall not covet your neighbor's wife" (Exod. 20:17). This commandment was not given by God just to regulate man's relationship with society in general, but to discipline the male in his greed and sexual lust. The man must work by the "sweat of his brow" to earn money, and trust God to take care of all of his needs; therefore, God said it was sin to covet his neighbor's money, possessions or wife.

This commandment does more than apply to the likes of property, i.e., "the ownership of things." This commandment extends to "the ownership of property," a basic plank in the Christian's orientation of life. A person is forbidden not only to take something that belongs to another, but even to desire or lust after such things. Specifically, a man is forbidden to desire the "stuff" or "wife of another man."

While some may think the wife listed here is part of the property of the house and nothing but chattel, this commandment recognizes the sexual lust of man, i.e., his propensity to rebel and satisfy his lust apart from God's plan.

But look at this commandment again even at its lowest plain; the wife is a member of the family and an essential element of the family, and this commandment is more than prohibiting sex; it's prohibiting a man from lusting after the companionship, abilities or any other asset of another man's wife.

An Ordered Birth Rate

God so ordered the family that throughout the world there is an even number of births between male and female children.

There may be the odd time when there may be more of one sex born than another, but over a long period of time the ratio has always evened itself out. He who controls all life—the introduction into life through birth, and the departure from life through death—has planned for an equal number of women and men to populate the world, hence laying a foundation for families to carry on the human race. In essence the law of intelligent design determined that the halves should be devoted to the whole.

Jesus' View of Marriage

When Jesus came into the world, He did not speak extensively about the family, or raising children, or principles for reproduction and perpetuity of the family. Jesus recognized the Old Testament law and reinforced what was originally taught in the Old Testament. He said, "Do not think that I came to destroy the Law or the Prophets. I did not come to destroy but to fulfill" (Matt. 5:17). Therefore, Jesus reinforced the family.

Jesus' main commission was for salvation, "For the Son of Man has come to save that which was lost" (Matt. 18:11). Again He said, "I did not come to call the righteous, but sinners" (Matt. 9:13). He came to make right that which was wrong, i.e., man's view of salvation. What was already right—the family— He supported the continuity of.

If a child had asked Jesus what relationship he should have to his earthly father, no doubt Jesus would have referred him to the law. The same if a man or a woman asked what was their relationship to one another. Again, Jesus would have referred them back to the teaching of the Old Testament.

When Paul laid the foundations for Christian actions in the newly founded church, he said, "Children, obey your parents in the Lord, for this is right. 'Honor your father and mother,' which is the first commandment with promise: 'that it may be well with you and you may live long on the earth'" (Eph. 6:1-3). Obviously, Paul supported the family principles of the Old Testament. He told wives to submit to their own husbands, and husbands to love their own wives as Christ loved the church, and to submit to each other (see Eph. 5:21-25).

The church is spoken of as the bride of Christ (see Eph. 5:24-27), and as such will be married in the future to the bridegroom, Jesus Christ. This picture of the New Testament church is reflective of the earthly institution of the family.

The Church Is Family

In one sense, each local church is a picture of the family of God, while the broader Body of Christ, i.e., the universal church, is also the family of God, which is composed of all believers in this dispensation.

To enter God's family, the believer must be "born again" or "born from above" (John 3:3-5). As such, each person realizes that God is his or her Father (see 1 Tim. 5:1), and they now belong to the "household of God" (Eph. 2:19). It's also called the "household of faith" (Gal. 6:10). In this family, the Christian refers to others as either his "brothers" or "sisters."

In the family, the Christian must show kindly affection to one another with "brotherly love" (Rom. 12:10). The author of Hebrews said, "Let brotherly love continue" (Heb. 13:1). And again, Peter said, "Love the brotherhood" (1 Pet. 2:17), and

"Love as brothers" (1 Pet. 3:8). Love as you would love family members, i.e., brotherly love, should be the badge or hallmark of every Christian (see John 13:35).

Local Church Ministries

Most churches have some type of family ministry to biological family units and to the larger local church family. The basis: when individuals learn to function in their biological family, they function better in their spiritual family. So the church teaches its members to live for Christ in families so they will be strengthened individually and the church body will be strengthened.

First, most churches provide useful *information* about parenting through pamphlets, newsletters, audiotapes, CDs, DVDs, retreats, seminars and regular topics in existing classes or through sermons. A lending library is important to supply these resources.

Second, *events* are designed for parents and children to participate together: movies to enhance family life, game night, family retreats, craft night and other family-oriented activities.

Third, churches provide all types of *counseling* that deal with short-term crises and long-term difficulties. The church can provide qualified counselors or point needy families to qualified Christian counselors.[6]

Fourth the church provides *enrichment*. This can be done by making the congregation aware of the kinds of pressures on the typical family, and how each person can support his or her family as well as encourage other families. Help can be tailored couple to couple or family to family, or involve preparing singles for marriage and equipping expecting couples to deal with their future parenting responsibility. Because most American families do not have an extended family nearby, the church becomes the surrogate extended family.

Fifth, the church can focus attention and provide resources for each family to have a *family altar*. That's a time when they pray together, read and/or study Scriptures together and meditate on God's presence. The old adage is still true, "The family that prays together, stays together."

Sixth, the church can foster *intergenerational activities*. Yes, a church may have an age-graded Sunday School, but there may be occasions when the family is kept together and taught together. The family can learn the necessity of strong families and learn this lesson all together. On that occasion, emphasize the *family pew* (perhaps on Mother's Day or Father's Day). Instead of delegating the kids to children's church and/or youth church in some other part of the church building, have families sit together (my church has a father and son, or grandfather and grandson choir on Father's Day).

Seventh is the creation of *special institutions* to deal with perceived social problems arising from adverse influences of public school: the creation of Christian schools to teach traditional family values or provide a solid academic education. There are 33,740 private schools in the United States, serving 6 million PK-12 students. Private schools account for more than 25 percent of the nation's schools and enroll about 11 percent of all students. Most private school students (81 percent) attend religiously affiliated schools.[7] Many other parents homeschool their children, with the aim of preserving the traditional Christian home. "Today, as a general idea, most agree that the number of homeschooled children in the United States is somewhere between 900,000 and 2,000,000."[8]

The eighth movement is the *house church* movement. When children are educated in the home, they acquire home values. Since there is no central clearinghouse of statistics on the house church movement, no one knows how many house churches there are, nor how many are involved in the movement.[9]

Wrap Up

When the church rightly influences the family, it has a deep influence on society and the individual. Because the family is the *first* influence on the child who will eventually take its values and attitudes into the culture, and because the family has a continuing influence on individuals, the church helps to shape every area of life when it influences the family.

If our families disintegrate, no matter what the cause, that will have a disastrous influence on individuals that will in turn have negative consequences on society as a whole and on the church. On the other hand, when the church has a positive effect on the family, it demonstrates what's right with the church.

What's right with the church? Family focus!

When the Church Is Right on Multiracial Involvement

*Where there is neither Greek nor Jew, circumcised nor uncircumcised,
barbarian, Scythian, slave nor free, but Christ is all and in all.*

COLOSSIANS 3:11

*Jesus did not address His audience as members of any class, possessors
of any peculiar culture or as people of wealth, rank, education or
position. Jesus spoke to all alike, but that did not mean they were all
the same. Some were deeper in sin than others; some were shallow in
their understanding; but all were needy, and Jesus loved them. Each
hearer received a word from Jesus according to his or her particular
need. The sermons of Jesus are for all generations, for all classes, for
all stations in life, for all ages, including children, the rich, slaves and
soldiers. The sermons of Jesus are for you.*

ELMER TOWNS

God loves people of every race and language, and He wants everyone to be one Body "where there is neither Greek nor Jew, circumcised nor uncircumcised, barbarian, Scythian, slave nor free, but Christ is all and in all" (Col. 3:11). When the church is right on the race and cultural issues, it reflects the Body that God intended it to be.

David Anderson, a recent graduate of Moody Bible Institute, and a staff member of Willow Creek Community Church, came to Columbia, Maryland, to begin an intentional, non-denominational multicultural church called Bridgeway Community Church. David Anderson later became an author on race relations and reached out to all people, to meet all needs and to be the bridge over multicultural and multiethnic barriers.

Today, more than 2,000 people attend the church's two morning services, where creative arts are used to reach people with practical Christian teaching, no matter where they may be on their spiritual journey. The worship service is called, "A Celebration of All Colors and Cultures Doing Life Together and Worshiping God Together."[1]

The church began on Easter Sunday of 1992, when Anderson met in people's homes. They sang without instruments and shared the gospel with coworkers. They shared the vision of Bridgeway, and immediately God moved in this little church and lives were changed. The cultural and racial blend has raised interest around the country in Bridgeway Church as it successfully fulfills its vision "to become a multicultural army of fully devoted followers of Christ, moving forward in unity and love to reach our community, our culture, and our world for Jesus Christ."[2]

The congregation is about 55 percent African American, 30 percent white and 15 percent Asian and other races. As David Anderson says in his book *Multicultural Ministry: Finding Your Church's Unique Rhythm*:

> Evidence of this country's rich racial mix is all around us, in our schools, our stores, our neighborhoods, our recreational facilities—everywhere except our churches. Heaven may include every culture, every tongue, and tribe, but in the United States, Sunday morning remains one of the last bastions of ethnic separation. It's time to stop merely talking about multicultural worship and start living it.[3]

Easier Said than Done

I have preached in many African-American churches, probably in at least a dozen states, and I have seen a congregation of black faces looking at me; they are not integrated. The same can be said for multitudes of white congregations. I've preached in all 50 of the United States, and I remember seeing a sea of white faces staring at me as I preach. They were not integrated.

And yet, because the issue of racism is approached from both sides, many times the African American fits very comfortably into a white congregation and the same happens when the reverse is followed. So what can we say? The church must do far more than state its intention in order to be successfully multiethnic or multicultural.

165

Because most neighborhood or family churches (attendance under 100) are primarily a single-cell church, it's very easy to understand why they are exclusively one ethnic group. The small church is defined as, "Everyone knows everyone, everyone relates to everyone, and everyone waits on everyone, before anyone will do anything."[4]

The term "multiracial" indicates the presence of many different races in a church. That's easy to achieve where people from all different races come and sit in a common worship service. However, the term "multicultural" emphasizes different racial groups bringing their culture into the worship service—into the choir, pulpit, communities and the whole way they do church.

One of the great churches of America that has been the most successful in breaking through culture barriers is the Brooklyn Tabernacle, known for its Grammy Award-winning multiracial choir. It is very sensitive to the several cultures attending each service from Brooklyn, New York. It can be said that the racial makeup of the church represents the racial makeup of the community.

Another church that has done an exemplary job integrating cultures is The Church On The Way, in Van Nuys, California, where Jack Hayford was the senior pastor for more than three decades. Today, Pastor Jim Tolle, the former pastor to the Hispanic congregation, is senior pastor of the church. Because the neighborhood is becoming multiethnic, no longer the white bedroom community of the Hollywood film industry, the church is reflecting the change that's happening in its neighborhood.

The church's facilities are used by Arab-speaking, Arian, Bulgarian, Hispanic and Filipino congregations. On any given weekend, there are four English-speaking services on one campus, five Spanish-speaking services on the other campus. Pastor Jim Tolle, having been a child of missionary parents and an adult missionary himself in several Latin American communities, is both bilingual and bicultural. The Spanish-language congregation has a higher attendance than the English-language congregations. This is a radical change from the early days when Jack Hayford came to an only English-speaking congregation, in a neighborhood that was primarily Anglo.

The Church On The Way, like many intentional multicultural churches, has written the race issues into its statement of ministry: "Radical harmony in God's Kingdom (see 1 Cor. 12:13; Gal. 3:27-29; Eph. 2:11-22; Col. 3:10-11) under God our Creator, ethnic diversity is respected; under Christ our redeemer, all humanity is invited to answer the Bible's call to the values and virtues of the Kingdom of God."[5]

Multicultural Churches Are Not the Same as Multiracial Churches

Most of the churches that identify themselves as multiethnic do not manifest as multicultural. People of different races attend, but there is typically one predominant culture in the worship services.

As an example, there can be a group of young adults who are Asian, Hispanic, African American and Anglo, all at the same church, all young professionals. They work together, listen to the same music, go to the same restaurants and are actually part of the same culture—regardless of their skin color. However, the worship service does not reflect the Asian styles of relationship or the African styles of worship or the Hispanic approaches to music. Though some people may call it a multicultural church, it probably is just a multiethnic church.

The Problem Outside America

In November 1978, I visited every refugee camp along the Mekong River in Thailand, along with a group of 22 other leaders and students from Liberty University. We were delivering food, blankets, Bibles and Christmas toys to thousands of refugees coming out of Laos, Cambodia and Vietnam. The Thailand government gathered them up and herded them into camps that looked like "concentration camps" of the World War II variety. These refugees had retreated from Vietnam, Laos and Cambodia after the American protective shield was removed and America withdrew from the South Asian nations, allowing the Communists to take over Vietnam. Thousands fled to Thailand for safety, and many nations had joined in humanitarian efforts to help preserve their lives.

I arrived a day earlier, hired an interpreter for the day and began walking through the refugee camp of 12,000 people, trying to write stories of Christians and churches I found in the refugee camp. I found a number of Christian church buildings, each one reflecting different cultures of the varying ethnic groups from the various nations. Each church building was vastly different, representing a different way of life, a different way of worship and the different values of the people.

I remember one building on stilts built completely out of bamboo, just the way it had been built back in the swamps of the jungle, only here there was no water. There was no reason to build the church high on stilts, for they were on the side of a hill, not in a swamp. But they followed their tradition.

Another church that represented the mountain tribes of Laos had cut down huge trees, dragged them into the refugee compound to use as benches and made this church look like home, just like the one back in the mountains.

As I walked through the churches, examining different kinds of literature, I found sources from Scripture Press, from Wheaton, Illinois; Christian Missionary Alliance, from New York; Baptist literature, from London, England; and Pentecostal literature from Springfield, Missouri. Christians in that part of the world are a clear minority, and their places of worship are recognizable, even when they are as different as slender bamboo or huge logs.

Later that evening, as I walked through the compound, I noticed the vast difference in worship styles. The mountain tribe from Laos was loud, bombastic even, and later they got louder. The bamboo church was quiet and meditative; I could barely hear their singing.

There are general principles that make a church multiracial. George A. Yancey examined the research from a Lilly Endowment study of multiracial churches across the United States, and in his book *One Body, One Spirit: Principles of Successful Multiracial Churches* wrote about what makes a church multiracial:

It must have a worship style inclusive of multiple cultures.
It must have ethnically diverse leadership.
It must have an overarching goal to become multiracial.
It must intentionally want to become multiracial.
It must have leadership with appropriate personal skills.

It must be in a location that can draw multiple races.
It must demonstrate an adaptability to overcome various challenges that arise.[6]

Pearl S. Buck, missionary to China before World War II, said, "Race prejudice is not only a shadow over the colored—it is a shadow over all of us, and the shadow is darkest over those who feel it least and allows its evil effects to go on."[7]

On the other side of racial prejudice comes a different quotation from twentieth-century African-American writer Zora Neale Hurston: "Sometimes I feel discriminated against, but it does not make me angry. It merely astonishes me. How they can deny themselves the pleasure of my company is beyond me!"

What the Bible Teaches

The Bible teaches clearly that God has made all men equal. When the church was first formed in the book of Acts, there were those Judaizers who wanted everyone to become like them—a Jew—before they could become a Christian. They wanted everyone to be circumcised, according to the manner of the Old Testament. But God had established a new dispensation, and the Body of Christ would be made up of people from all cultures, they would share equally, and be accepted by God equally.

The racial impasse came when "certain *men* came down from Judea (to Antioch) and taught the brethren, 'Unless you are circumcised according to the custom of Moses, you cannot be saved'" (Acts 15:1).

If the Judaizers had won the day, the church would forever be small and the purpose of God blunted in the world. But at the Jerusalem Council (see Acts 15), Peter stood up to declare that God had "given them [Gentiles] the Holy Spirit, just as *He did* to us, and made no distinction between us and them, purifying their hearts by faith" (Acts 15:8-9). The good news is that the Council agreed with Peter, and the church tore down any racial barrier, meaning that all who accepted Jesus Christ were accepted equally.

Later, when Paul went to preach on Mars Hill in Athens, Greece, he reiterated a Christian's position toward racial equality when he said, "He [God] gives to all life, breath, and all things. And He has made from one blood every nation of men to dwell on all the face of the earth" (Acts 17:25-26).

Did you take note of the words "one blood"? To the shame of America and the Red Cross, when blood transfusions were made at the beginning of World War II, the blood donated from whites was kept separate from the blood donated from African Americans. Thanks to the work of an African-American doctor, Charles Richard Drew, we came to understand that blood is the same in all people.[8] America finally realized what God had said all along—that the world had one blood.

Even though people like to criticize the American church and call it "the most segregated hour of the week," the church has been right in this issue much more than it's been wrong. Missionaries have gone to all tribes, cultures and languages, preaching Jesus Christ equally and without bias.

Great Christian churches have been built around the world, among all nations and languages; and when there was only one ethnic group in a nation, they made up that church. Where there have been multiethnic groups of people, they have formed multiethnic churches. Why? Because the church of Jesus Christ has been colorblind to the appearance of a man's skin. Here is what the church believes:

- All are created in the image of God (see Gen. 1:27).
- All have sinned and come short of the glory of God (see Rom. 3:23).
- Jesus died for all (see 2 Cor. 5:15).
- All can be saved and be a full member of the Body of Christ (see 1 Cor. 12:27).
- All are fellow workers in the mission of Jesus Christ on this earth (see Col. 4:11).

Concerns

America is not the only nation to have a race problem among its peoples. When you begin to look at the world as a whole, the Thai and Vietnamese have usually resented the Cambodian. And the Koreans find it difficult to get along with the Japanese, perhaps because of the military occupation of Japan at the first part of the nineteenth century, but also because of the differences in their cultural attitudes, even though they both are called "Asian." And then again, there has always been hatred between Iraq and Iran (going back to Old Testament times when they were called Persia and Babylon), even though both are Middle Eastern nations, and both represent Arab cultures.

Therefore, let's realize that to become multiracial and multicultural is always difficult, but when Christ comes in, "there is neither Greek nor Jew, circumcised nor uncircumcised, barbarian, Scythian, slave *nor* free, but Christ *is* all and in all" (Col. 3:11, emphasis added).

Many Americans have seen television images of racism in the last 100 years. Some older Americans will remember the "whites only" drinking fountains, while young Americans have seen only equality on television. Between these two generations, most realize there have been past difficulties, but they know that the bicultural barrier must be bridged. The problem is that many just don't want to do it.

Is this an historical matter? In some cases. Is it a preference matter? Does it mean that some Anglos don't relate well to an African-American culture, and does it mean the same when the reverse is seen?

As a result, it is not always a group's preference to worship in a culture that is different from their own. If worship comes from the deep recesses of the heart, where a man is honest before God and his brothers, then most people will worship best in their own cultural expression. But don't miss my point: racism, segregation and prejudice are sin.

The flashpoint of racial divide is usually leadership. A culture determines how much and what style of leadership will be practiced in each different cultural setting. That's where the problem must be solved. First, there are biblical requirements for church leadership; second, there are cultural requirements, and the way people interpret the two is not always the same.

If worship was the great divide, then it would seem like when we worship together we solve our problems. Remember the old chorus sung before Communion, "Let us break bread together on our knees . . ."? That means that all of us are equal when we bow our knee to God. The problem is that many churches fail to move beyond worship. They don't make a connection between worship styles in the church and styles of leadership in the church or styles of fellowship.

The Making of a Great College

When Jerry Falwell and I founded Liberty University, we began an unusual college. It was not going to be an interdenominational college, nor was it going to be a college that belonged to a denomination or fellowship. I told Jerry, "Let's start with the premise that our college will be an extension of the local church at the collegiate level." He bought into that idea, so I added, "Everything that a church does to influence its members, a church college would do to influence college students."

So, from day one, we planned that every student at Liberty University would join Thomas Road Baptist Church, work in Thomas Road Baptist Church and become a full, active member of Thomas Road Baptist Church. But because of the past segregation issues, Thomas Road Baptist Church had never baptized or accepted a black member into its congregation. I remember telling Jerry Falwell, "We can't have racial prejudice and become a great university to touch the world."

Jerry agreed with me. He agreed that we would accept an African-American adult into Thomas Road Baptist Church in the summer of 1971. He realized that certain white members of the church would leave when he did, but he was prepared to make that decision because it was the right thing to do.

John Maxwell once said, "Choose who you lose." It's not wrong to lose some people; as a matter of fact, some churches are healthier when they lose certain people. This was certainly the case at Thomas Road Baptist.

To the day of his death, Jerry Falwell and I argued over who baptized the first African-American member of Thomas Road Baptist Church. In those days, I was doing some of the baptizing; I volunteered to baptize a young African-American 22-year-old male who was leaving Lynchburg to go into the U.S. Air Force.

I told Jerry that if the church rebelled and refused to follow the concept of a multiracial college, he could always fire me, and the church and college could go on. I was willing to make that sacrifice because it was the right thing to do.

I remember standing in the baptistery and announcing to the church that the young man was becoming a member of Thomas Road Baptist Church and would be leaving to go into the military. Then I asked the church to accept him: "Everyone who is glad to receive

The story of Thomas Road Baptist Church is given to illustrate how many churches struggle with incorporating people of a different race into the local body. The exclusion of others from different backgrounds is understandable, because a church has people who know everyone, relate to everyone and respect everyone. What is not acceptable is when a church knowingly excludes anyone on the basis of race, culture or age. The illustration of Thomas Road Baptist Church suggests how many thousands of churches have overcome prejudices because they obey the commands of Jesus to go preach to everyone, win everyone, baptize everyone (into your fellowship), and then involve them in ministry.

my brother, and will pray for him as he leaves Lynchburg and goes into the Air Force, and pray that God would use him greatly in the ministry . . . say 'amen.'"

There was an abundance of "amens" in the church to show they fully accepted this new standard. Thus, because of Christ and the Great Commission, the color barrier was broken at Thomas Road Baptist Church.

Jerry's Apology

In 1979, the Moral Majority was announced, and shortly thereafter, Jesse Jackson, the civil rights worker from Chicago, Illinois, came to Lynchburg to preach at Court Street Baptist Church, denouncing the Moral Majority. That night, Jerry Falwell called my home to ask me to go with him to the meeting, but I was out of town. He ended up calling Dr. Carl Diemer, a professor of church history, and the two of them went down to Court Street Baptist Church, which is known throughout the area as a former slave church.

The church was packed with people standing around the walls when Jerry Falwell walked in a few minutes before the meeting started. He walked down the center aisle, turned to his left and asked two young men to go stand against the wall. He sat on the front row waiting to hear the criticism of Jesse Jackson against the Moral Majority.

A young man came out from the back room to a silent audience and said, "Dr. Falwell, what are you doing here?"

"I heard Jesse Jackson was going to preach against the Moral Majority," Jerry replied, "and I came to find out what he had to say."

The emissary took Jerry's message to the back room. Shortly, he came back and said that Jesse Jackson wanted to meet Jerry. In that back room, Jerry and Jesse shook hands and became life-long good friends, although they each held to their own opinions. Jerry asked if he could have five minutes to address the audience that night. "I'll give you five minutes to speak on the 'Old Time Gospel Hour' on Sunday," he told Jesse. The two men again shook hands.

Dr. Falwell stood before the audience and said, "You all know that I am a product of a segregated South. You all know that I have said things against the African American, and I am ashamed of what I said . . ." That night Jerry Falwell apologized from the pulpit for his racial remarks; he apologized for his racial actions in the city; and he asked humbly for the African-American community to forgive him.

There were several African-American men in the audience that night who heard Falwell and later verified the story I am now telling. At the end, Falwell said, "It's easy to say 'I am sorry', but you have to prove it; a person has to say 'I'm sorry' with actions." Then Falwell added, "I am offering free tuition to any African-American pastor who lives within driving distance of Lynchburg to come to Liberty University and receive his education."

Reverend Carlton Jackson, pastor of Pleasant Valley Baptist Church in East Lynchburg, Virginia, was there that evening and took Jerry Falwell up on his promise. He graduated from Liberty University and has pastored Pleasant Valley Baptist Church for 25 years, since 1984.

Over the years, Liberty University has had a larger percentage of African-American students than any other traditionally white university in the state of Virginia. But just numbers are not enough; there are African-American faculty, vice presidents, coaches and board members.

I am an habitual counter. Sometimes when I'm listening to a university singing group, and I get lost in the words, I count the number of African-American students and divide into the total number of singers. Whereas approximately 11 percent of Americans are African American, it always pleases me when I see a larger percentage of African Americans in our singing groups, or in other groups.

Liberty University is multiethnic, not because it's politically correct or because it's a civil rights issue, but because it marches to the drumbeat of the Great Commission. Jesus told us to go to all . . . to preach the gospel to all . . . to baptize all . . . and Liberty has carried out that Commission. There are many great African-American pastors in America who received their training at Liberty, and I am proud of every one of them.

Wrap Up

If all our churches were to become multicultural and multiethnic, that would not solve the evils of the church. There are many things wrong with the church, and they are found in the deep attitudes of the heart that usually are hidden. However, when the church is right in its heart toward the multiracial and multicultural, then the church is right in a crucial area of biblical ethics.

There is no greater witness for God than when He looks at His great worshiping Body and sees those from "every tribe and tongue and people and nation" (Rev. 5:9).

Let's make it our prayer that more churches will become like the scene from heaven, filled with men and women from every tribe, tongue and nation, singing around the throne.

You are worthy to take the scroll,
And to open the seals;
   For You were slain,
And have redeemed us to God by Your blood
   Out of every tribe and tongue and people and nation,
And have made us kings and priests to our God;
   And we shall reign on the earth (Rev. 5:9-10).

If we could see men and women from every tribe and language and culture worshiping together on earth, maybe we would be better prepared for heaven when we get there.

What's right with the church? The church is right when it takes down racial and cultural barriers.

WHEN THE CHURCH IS RIGHT ON THE GREAT COMMISSION

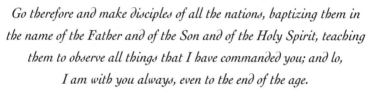

Go therefore and make disciples of all the nations, baptizing them in the name of the Father and of the Son and of the Holy Spirit, teaching them to observe all things that I have commanded you; and lo, I am with you always, even to the end of the age.

MATTHEW 28:19-20 ·

No one has the right to hear the gospel twice, while there remains someone who has not heard it once.

OSWALD J. SMITH

We talk of the Second Coming; half the world has never heard of the first.

OSWALD J. SMITH

Unlike all other religions, Christianity is not about simply learning doctrine and rules, then passing what is learned from generation to generation. Each follower of Christ is obligated to become vitally involved in carrying out the Great Commission directly or indirectly to everyone in the entire world. When the church gets the Great Commission right, it can impact the world.

Other religions teach doctrine and rules and offer their own solution for the universal sin problem. They all offer a unique way to go to "heaven" after a person dies. But one does not become a Christian simply by learning doctrine and following rules. Christianity is a relationship with a Person, Jesus Christ. When He lives in the heart of a believer, that person wants to obey the commands Jesus gave when He was alive. Jesus told His disciples (and us) to love God with all our heart (the Great Commandment) and to carry His gospel to all the world (the Great Commission).

In 1956, five young missionaries (three from Wheaton College; the pilot; and Roger Youdarian, who had gone to Northwestern College with me in Minneapolis-St. Paul, Minnesota) were trying to evangelize the Huaorani Indians, referred to by the media and in this story as the Auca Indians in Ecuador, South America. Now, you might ask why college-educated young people would bury their lives in the jungles of South America, especially when they had so much going for them. Also, why this tribe? Later studies show that the Ecuadorian government had determined to eliminate the Aucas because of their fierceness to other tribes and their resistance to every endeavor to civilize them.

These five young men used a yellow Piper Cruiser airplane to reach out to the Aucas and other tribes with the gospel. They planned to land the Piper Cruiser on a sandbar in the middle of the Curaray River in the dry season, before the winter floods covered their landing strip. In what is called pre-evangelism, the five young men left gifts to make friends with the tribes, but the Indians didn't understand their friendship. When the young men settled in to spend their first night among the Auca Indians, all five were speared and then hacked with machetes.

Throughout history, it is said that the blood of martyrs becomes the seed of the church. More than 250,000 martyrs died under Roman persecution in the first 200 years of Christianity. Christianity exploded in outreach after Constantine adopted Christianity in A.D. 312 and began the process of making it an official religion of the Roman Empire.

God honored the faith of these five men, and eventually the gospel was preached to the tribe, and many became Christians. In August 2000, I heard Mincaye[1] speak at the Billy Graham conference on evangelism in Amsterdam. He admitted to being one of those who killed the missionaries. Mincaye testified that he was now an elder in the church and had been evangelizing other communities.

Rachel Saint, sister of the martyred Nate Saint, was so convinced that the tribe needed to be reached that she went back to raise her children among those people. Her influence, plus that of many other missionaries, spread the gospel among the Auca Indians.[2] Note that Rachel didn't run back to the United

States in bitterness and grief, but rather, she wanted to make sure that the death of her brother would have eternal results among the people he had attempted to reach.

Why was she so determined? Because she served the living Lord, who had sent her brother to the Auca Indians. She also knew that her brother's reward was not in this life but in the next. She wanted to continue the Great Commission that her brother had attempted to carry out.

The Auca Indians' language was reduced to writing, and the New Testament was translated into the language so the people could be taught to read the Word of God. Today there's a thriving church among the Auca Indians, and the Ecuadorian government recognizes the advanced civilization of the Auca Indians.

So, why would five young men risk their lives to preach the gospel? The reason is because Jesus commanded His followers to preach the good news to every person (see Mark 16:15). Ask yourselves a second question: *Why would Rachel Saint's young son, Steve, then spend his life transforming the pagan Auca culture into one with Christian values?* Because Jesus commanded, "teaching them to observe all things that I have commanded you" (Matt. 28:20).

A Command to Reach All Peoples of All Decades

Let's go back to the first century to see how the Great Commission was communicated to Jesus' apostles after He was raised from the dead.

When Jesus first appeared to 10 disciples in the Upper Room on Easter Sunday afternoon, He gave them a simple command: "As the Father has sent Me, I also send you" (John

20:21). Jesus didn't tell them where to go or what to do; nor did He tell them what message they should preach. His message was simply, "Go."

The example of the Great Commission was Jesus Himself. As He had been sent into the world, He was going to send them into the world. In the following week, Jesus would tell them what they must do.

A week later, Jesus met His disciples again in the Upper Room and began to explain the Great Commission further: "Go into all the world and preach the gospel to every creature" (Mark 16:15). They were not to return to Galilee and preach to Jews only, but to go to all people in the world, and preach to everyone. This commission was surely "great" compared to anything they had thought previously.

Approximately two weeks later, Jesus met the disciples again in Galilee on a mountain (see Matt. 28:16). Here He gave them a strategy of how they would carry out the Great Commission: "Go therefore and make disciples of all the nations, baptizing them in the name of the Father and of the Son and of the Holy Spirit, teaching them to observe all things that I have commanded you; and lo, I am with you always, even to the end of the age" (Matt. 28:19-20).

The word "go" is actually a participle that could be translated "as you are going." This means Jesus assumed they would obey the command He had previously given. The imperative in the sentence is the command, "Make disciples." A person became a follower of Jesus Christ when he became a disciple, so Jesus wanted them to get everyone else in the world to follow Him also.

But it is not enough only to become a follower of Jesus; they had to be baptized by a Trinitarian formula—"in the name of the Father, the Son and the Holy Spirit." It was not enough just to add them to a church role; each new convert had to obey what Jesus had taught them, "teaching them to observe all things that I have commanded you" (Matt. 28:20).

What Happened to the Twelve?

As the first century of the Early Church came to an end, history tells us that the 12 apostles went everywhere preaching the Word, just as Jesus told them. Tradition tells us that they divided up the known world, and they did as Jesus commanded, taking the gospel "to the end of the earth" (Acts 1:8).

Church history tells us that Andrew went to Asia Minor, which is modern Turkey, and then traveled up near the Black Sea, which is modern southern Russia. He eventually was crucified in Achaia. Because Andrew felt unworthy to die on the same type of cross on which Jesus died, they bound him to an x-shaped cross, and that cross has been preserved in the national flag of Scotland as the St. Andrew's cross.

The apostle Philip also ministered in Eastern Turkey and then journeyed from there to the nation of Gaul, which is today France. He's the only one of the 12 to go to France, and he was stoned for his faith then crucified in Hieropolis.

Bartholomew, also the one called Nathaniel, went to Armenia and started the church in that nation. Some historians say that Armenia was the first nation to become thoroughly Christian. Then he went on to Albania, where he was beaten and crucified.

Church historians claim that Thomas went to India, and today there is strong Indian tradition that the Mar Thoma Church of India was founded by this disciple in A.D. 52. They say he landed at Cranganore and was instrumental in the conversion of many high-caste Indian families. As he continued pushing to the regions beyond, he was martyred in Mylapore on the coast of India.

Matthew went to Ethiopia and probably died in Egypt, martyred by the Sanhedrin there. James the son of Alpheus went to Syria and was eventually martyred in Jerusalem.

Simon the Zealot went across North Africa, preaching the gospel and establishing churches, and then went up the Atlantic Coast of Europe as far as Britain. He returned to the Promised Land and then traveled into Syria, where he was captured and sawn in half.

Judas Thaddeus preached the gospel in Edessa and Armenia and was killed with arrows at the foot of Mount Ararat.

The 12 apostles obeyed the commands of Jesus, just as the five martyrs in Ecuador, and just as thousands of other followers of Jesus have done. The passion was not to become a martyr, but rather to win as many people to Christ as possible. Obviously, the negative side of that passion was so that people might not die and go to hell; and for that passion, many have been martyred.

The Early Church understood the Great Commission mandate: "Daily in the temple, and in every house, they did not cease teaching and preaching Jesus as the Christ" (Acts 5:42). That means they went into the homes, the marketplaces, the synagogues, the jails; and they preached before rulers, kings and the religious Sanhedrin. Everywhere they went, they told the story of Jesus Christ. They did it so often that the Jews complained, "You have filled Jerusalem with your doctrine" (Acts 5:28).

But they didn't just preach the gospel in Jerusalem. When Paul ended up in Rome, chained to a guard, he tried to win every soldier to Christ. As Paul won each guard to Christ, the gospel spread through the Roman soldiers to such an extent that he could say, "It has become evident to the whole palace guard, and to all the rest, that my chains are in Christ" (Phil. 1:13). Paul also noted that people had been saved in the palace, "especially those who are of Caesar's household" (Phil. 4:22). Perhaps this was the beginning of preaching the gospel in Caesar's palace so that 150 years later, Constantine, the Roman Emperor, became converted in A.D. 312.[3]

The Great Commission endeavor continued with Patrick, who went to Ireland to evangelize the entire nation. Then, on the Island of Iona, missionaries were trained and sent out to evangelize surrounding nations.[4] After the Protestant Reformation, first by Martin Luther in 1519, followed by John Calvin in Geneva from 1536 to 1538, the gospel continued to spread throughout Europe.[5]

Nowhere did evangelism burn brighter than under the influence of John Wesley, known for new "methods" from whence the movement was called Methodists. An early painting of John Wesley showed him in front of a globe. Across the bottom was the writing, "The world, my parish." Within a generation after John Wesley died, the Methodist Church became the largest Protestant movement in the world.

Nowhere was the Methodist outreach more prevalent than in the United States. During the War of 1776, there were 242 Methodist churches; and by the War of 1812, there were more than

5,000 Methodist churches, perhaps the greatest explosion of church planting in the history of Christianity.

As the young nation was pushing out in every direction, so were circuit-riding Methodist preachers, explorers and pioneers. Peter Cartwright was converted in the Cane Ridge Revival (Kentucky), in 1800, where the Second Great Awakening started.[6] He would return home at night filled with drinking and dancing, but suddenly conviction gripped his soul and for weeks he "prayed through" but couldn't find peace until his mother prayed with him.

At age 19, he began with an "exhorter's license" and a circuit in Western Kentucky whereby he rode out for 40 or 50 miles, covering one side of the county, and returned on a county road on the other side of the county to his home, 27 days later. Cartwright was a shouting Methodist, as were most of the circuit-riding preachers. Going down a lonely, deserted country road, he would shout and sing songs of Zion at the top of his voice to attract attention. When people came to the road, he gathered them into tobacco barns, stables, kitchens or county inns and preached the gospel to them. When people were converted, he organized them into a Methodist church and promised to be back within four weeks. These were called quarter-time churches.

Peter Cartwright would plant about 40 churches in his 27-day circuit. As property was donated, log churches were built; and within time, laymen were called to the ministry and became pastors of the congregations. When Cartwright finished planting 40 churches in one county, he went to another county to plant another 40 churches. Such was the Great Commission

189

passion of Peter Cartwright and thousands of other Methodist missionaries like him. What circuit-riding Methodist preachers did in the United States, young missionaries also went out from Christian colleges in America and Europe to go around the world to plant churches.

William Carey (1761–1834) is called the "Father of Modern Missions." Born in England, as a boy he learned Dutch, French, Greek, Hebrew and Latin. When preaching at a ministerial meeting on foreign mission, the moderator told him, "Sit down, young man. When God sees fit to convert the heathen, He will do it of His own accord." Carey went to India, and in spite of severe obstacles, he translated the Bible into 44 languages and dialects of India. The church he planted still exists in India (I visited it in 1978 for prayer meeting).[7]

In 1910, the Student Volunteer Movement had a great convention in Edinburgh, Scotland, with more than 1,200 young people attending. The Edinburgh Missionary Conference motivated hundreds to go to the mission field. The 1800s and 1900s showed great missionary advances for the cause of Christ.

Even in modern times, the Great Commission has been and is being carried out by many other individuals. During World War II, Dawson Trotman began the Navigators, a networking system reaching primarily among U.S. Navy sailors to win and make disciples of these young men, of which thousands came to know Jesus Christ. After the war, they returned home to be trained in Bible colleges and seminaries. Those who were Navigators, and thousands of others, went back to foreign mission fields where they served during the war. There were almost 100,000 missionaries in the golden years after World War II.

About the same time, Bill Bright felt called as a missionary to the college campuses of America, beginning at UCLA in Greater Los Angeles, California. He began Campus Crusade for Christ, and the power of this movement spread to other college campuses all over the world. Beginning at the major colleges, working down to smaller colleges and then to community colleges, Campus Crusade currently is served by more than 25,000 full-time staff and more than 553,000 volunteer workers in 196 countries in areas that represent 99.6 percent of the world's population and is comprised of 70 special ministries, one of the largest evangelical mission forces in the world.[8]

Perhaps one of the best-known local churches to support foreign missions is People's Church of Toronto, Canada. Begun by Oswald J. Smith in 1920, in a tent meeting, Smith promoted a "bring your own chair" night and filled the tent with "every kind of kitchen chair imaginable." From that they built an 1,800-seat auditorium. Between 1920 and 1959, the church raised $14 million for missions. This was the first church in the world to give $1 million a year to missions, and later it was the first to give $2 million a year to missions.

The Canadian Prairies were known as the "bread basket" of North America for all the wheat grain grown there. But the prairies were the spiritual bread basket of the world as well. In the three prairie provinces there were only three million people but more than 60 Bible institutes and colleges. When young people got their education, they would get on the Canadian National train, go to Toronto, get financial support from The People's Church and go to the jungles of the world. Probably no church has supported more foreign missions than The People's Church.

Smith was known for visiting missionaries, carrying money to them, and preaching great crusades where thousands of people were saved.

Individual Responsibility

Every Christian must face two questions from his local church. The first question is, *Why am I here?* This is another way of asking the question in reverse, *Why didn't God take me home when I got saved?* The answer is that God wants to use you as a testimony in your present surroundings, but He also wants you to share the gospel and take people with you to heaven.

> ### Missionary Statement
> By Oswald J. Smith
>
> - You must go or send a substitute.
> - Attempt great things for God, expect great things from God.
> - This generation can only reach this generation.
> - The light that shines for Christ, shines brightest at home.
> - Why should anyone hear the gospel twice before everyone has heard it once?[9]

The second question is, *What does Christ want me to do about carrying out the Great Commission?* The Great Commission has an obligation upon two recipients. First, the church must carry out the Great Commission to all the world, using all of its personnel, resources and energies. Second, each believer has a responsibility to do his or her part to help reach the world with the gospel.

First, let's look at how the local church is obliged to carry out the Great Commission. Jesus said that when someone is won to

Christ, they should be "baptized in the name of the Father, Son and Holy Spirit." This is a church ordinance and includes incorporating new believers into a local fellowship of believers. Therefore, the church is God's instrument to mobilize His people for carrying out the Great Commission in the whole world.

How will the local church do it? By praying for lost people, giving money to support missionaries, being involved in missionary projects, sending its young people as missionaries and focusing its attention on reaching the world for Jesus Christ before He comes back.

But there's a second recipient of that question. Every individual believer is responsible for the Great Commission. Whether we witness to our family when we're first saved or we try to win our friends to Jesus Christ, we should attempt to win those closest to us. We should be like a rock thrown into the middle of a pool where the ripples continue to go outward, influencing the larger society.

There are numerous churches that have given themselves to strong foreign missionary endeavors. When you walk into the foyer, you might see a large thermometer representing money being raised for missions. You might go past a bulletin board where you see pictures or names of all the missionaries supported by that church on the foreign field. When you go into the auditorium or another place in the church, you might see a large map of the world, reminding people of Jesus' command to "go into all the world."

The problem in America is that we have "building-centered evangelism." We want to invite people into our buildings to hear the gospel, or we want to gather them into a group where we can preach to them. However, when you think of the Great Commission, think of all the various methods God uses to reach the world: education evangelism, agricultural evangelism, radio evangelism, student evangelism, riverboat evangelism, church-planting evangelism, street-preaching evangelism, literature evangelism, Internet evangelism, prison evangelism, child evangelism, youth evangelism, Bible distribution, college dorm evangelism, and so on.

The Great Commission is carried out by churches, just as it was in New Testament times. First, the church was a *gathering Body*; secondly, it was a *scattering Body*. The church gathered people together for teaching, fellowship, worship and the encouragement of one another.

But then persecution came. Before Paul was converted, he persecuted the church in Jerusalem; what happened to the Christians? "Those who were scattered went everywhere preaching the word" (Acts 8:4). In the next few chapters of Acts, some believers went to Samaria, some went to Lebanon, some went to Antioch; but all took the gospel to every part of the surrounding world, thus carrying out the Great Commission.

Jesus gave us two parables that apply how missionary outreach takes place. In the parable of the wedding guest, Jesus speaks about inviting guests to attend a wedding feast (see Matt. 22:1-14). The servants were commanded to go and find people and invite them to the wedding feast. That's a picture of Jesus commanding us to go and invite others to hear the gospel.

In the second parable (see Luke 14:16-24), a rich man had planned a dinner party and invited many people to come. But when the guests did not show up, the host gave the command to his servants to go out and bring the people in (see Luke 14:21). Still, he didn't have enough people, so again he commanded, "Go out into the highways and hedges, and compel them to come in, that my house may be filled" (Luke 14:23). That's a picture of the church aggressively going outside its doors to where the people are, motivating them to salvation.

The Message

As people go out preaching to the lost, notice what message Jesus gives. When He first encountered the disciples fishing along the Sea of Galilee, He said, "Follow Me, and I will make you become fishers of men" (Mark 1:17, *KJV*). The first part of that command was to "follow." The second was to become "fishers of men." Therefore, the purpose of their evangelism was pointed at people. The Great Commission didn't include constructing buildings, classrooms, parking lots or all of the other "stuff" the church does to carry out the Great Commission. These are important, but only as a secondary means. The message is primary, and we use the secondary means to carry out the primary message.

When Jesus told His disciples to "go into all the world and preach the gospel to every creature" (Mark 16:15), He used the term "gospel." The word "gospel" is found 76 times in the New Testament. It's an old Anglo-Saxon word that meant "God spell," meaning "God's story." So what is the gospel? It is the story of God who came to earth as a babe, lived without sin but died for our sins so that we might go to heaven. That is the message we preach that will transform the world. Salvation is the Great Commission message.

When you see the word "evangelize," it means to announce or proclaim the good news. It occurs 51 times in the New Testament and is a verb form of the noun "gospel." So when a person evangelizes another, what is he doing? He is putting the gospel into the recipient's life. He *gospelizes* them.

Another word used for preaching is "witness." Jesus told His disciples, "And you shall be witnesses to Me in Jerusalem, and in all Judea and Samaria, and to the end of the earth" (Acts 1:8). The focus of witnessing was a Person—Jesus Christ.

"Witness" is a legal term used in a trial. A witness was one who was expected to tell the truth concerning what he had seen, heard or experienced. A witness didn't interpret the circumstances, nor did he tell what he thought happened.

Once there was a television detective who used to say he wanted "just the facts." So a witness should tell "just the facts" concerning what Jesus has done for him or her. When someone witnesses about Jesus Christ, that person shares how he or she became a Christian, what Christ has done for him or her, and what Christ means to him or her now.

The word "witness" leads to another word: "testimony." That involves a person attesting to what Christ has done for him or her—how Christ has changed his or her life. That's why Jesus told His disciples, "You are witnesses of these things" (Luke 24:48).

A Christian should witness by the words he speaks, but also by the life that he lives. Christianity is not just about keeping rules; it's about an attitude behind the rules. The Christian should express the fruit of the Holy Spirit in his life, which is love, joy, peace, patience, gentleness, goodness, faith, meekness, and self-discipline (see Gal. 5:22-23). When a Christian is motivated and guided by the Holy Spirit—when the Holy Spirit is in control—that Christian shows other people what God can do in his life, i.e., he becomes a testimony to others. The ultimate goal of silent witnessing is to get other people to want Jesus Christ, which then opens up verbal witnessing.

Taking the Initiative

Because the message is compelling, people must believe it or they will be lost. Because winning the lost is compelling, the Christian is to obey the command of Jesus Christ to go and share the gospel. Every Christian must take the initiative to seek those who need to be saved and then share the gospel with them.

Remember, all evangelism eventually comes down to a one-on-one encounter between the person and Jesus Christ. They must have a one-on-one encounter with Him. If they sit in a group where they hear the gospel preached or taught, they must still have a one-on-one encounter with Jesus Christ. They must be saved individually and personally. Groups of people are never saved *en masse*; they are saved one at a time.

Jesus said, "I am the good shepherd. The good shepherd gives His life for the sheep" (John 10:11). The Christian must be like the shepherd; he must give his life to go seek lost people to tell them of the gospel.

Jesus told the parable of a man who had a hundred sheep, but one was lost. Did the man settle in for the night? No! He left the 99 sheep and went to find the one that was lost (see Luke 15:4). What happened when the shepherd found his lost sheep? Jesus said, "I say to you that likewise there will be more joy in heaven over one sinner who repents than over ninety-nine just persons who need no repentance" (Luke 15:7). How does that rejoicing take place? "And when he [the shepherd] comes home, he calls together his friends and neighbors, saying to them, 'Rejoice with me, for I have found my sheep which was lost!' " (Luke 15:6). That means Jesus rejoices with us when we win someone to Christ. Because Jesus is intentional about winning lost people to salvation, we too should be that intentional in reaching our friends and family.

Remember, there are many "lost sheep" who don't want to be found. They have hardened their hearts to the gospel; or they love their sin; or they, for one reason or another, have turned away from God. The Christian cannot do much about that. But he can pray that the Holy Spirit will soften the person's heart. And he can do deeds of kindness that will soften the person's heart. Jesus said, "The Son of Man did not come to be served, but to serve" (Mark 10:45). In the same way, we, as Christians, do not want unsaved people to serve us; we must serve them.

Wrap Up

The church has brought civilization to heathen tribes whose destructive ways destroyed themselves and others. But it never was a humanitarian effort, nor was it a peacekeeping effort. The message of Jesus Christ transforms individuals and lifts society to a higher level.

The church has sacrificed its money, its young people and its energy to evangelize the world. Why? Because people are lost, and Jesus told us to go tell them about salvation.

What's right with the church? Transforming lost people and heathen societies.

WHEN THE CHURCH IS
RIGHT ON THE FUTURE

⸻

*Looking for the blessed hope and glorious appearing of
our great God and Savior Jesus Christ.*

TITUS 2:13

*Science has found that nothing can disappear without a trace.
Nature does not know extinction. All it knows is transformation.
If God applies the fundamental principle to the most minute
and insignificant parts of the universe, doesn't it make sense
to assume that He applies it to the masterpiece of His creation —
the human soul? I think it does.*

DR. WERNHER VON BRAUN (1912–1977)

*When scientist Faraday was questioned on his speculations of
a life after death, he replied: "Speculations? I know nothing about
speculations. I'm resting on certainties. I know that my Redeemer
lives, and because He lives, I shall live also."*

MICHAEL FARADAY (1791–1867)

*Hope is one of the most powerful values known to mankind;
it transforms individuals and changes society. Jesus offered hope
after death: "I go to prepare a place for you . . . I will come again
and receive you to Myself" (John 14:2-3). People with hope live
with confidence and inspire others. But the church offers more
than hope after death; it teaches that God has a wonderful
plan for each individual in this life, and a blessed hope after
they die. When the church gets it right in its role in
offering future hope, it can influence society.*

Every person has a deep desire for life beyond death and a passion to live in a perfect place after the grave. Even some who deny the existence of hell believe there is a real place called heaven after death. Probably many people before Abraham longed for heaven, but he is the first described in Scripture as the one who "looked for a city which hath foundations, whose builder and maker is God" (Heb. 11:10, *KJV*). It's interesting to note that the Bible says Abraham didn't live in that city on earth, but he "died in faith" (Heb. 11:13). In a similar way, most Christians want to live a perfect life on this earth but know it won't happen. However, they have a great "hope" of living with God in heaven after death.

Jesus made certain promises about heaven on the night before He died. He told His disciples in the Upper Room very plainly that He was going away: "In My Father's house are many mansions. . . . I go to prepare a place for you" (John 14:2-3). While heaven is a real place for real people for a real eternity, the most important thing about heaven is not the place; it's the fact that Christians will live with God. Notice what Jesus promised: He "will come again and receive you to Myself; that where I am, *there* you may be also" (John 14:3). What's the most important thing in that verse? The word "myself." Jesus will come to take us to Himself.

Paul spoke about this event, calling it the "blessed hope." That describes Christ's return to receive Christians and take them to heaven to live with Him. Paul said, "Looking for the blessed hope and glorious appearing of our great God and Savior Jesus Christ" (Titus 2:13).

When Peter was writing, he also described it as "a living hope . . . to an inheritance incorruptible and undefiled . . . reserved in heaven for you" (1 Pet. 1:3-4). Why did Peter call this a *living hope*? Because in the heart of a Christian is an assurance that he will live for God; that assurance lives within the Christian's heart while he is on earth.

Some people wrongly think that heaven is just the good life here on earth. Other people think of heaven as golden streets, a stream of water and other earthly benefits. But the Bible says that it will be a "new heaven and a new earth" (Rev. 21:1).

Yet when the Bible speaks about the "new heaven and new earth," it says that there are at least three heavens. The first heaven is the atmosphere about us where air exists that is necessary for humans and all created life on this planet (see Matt. 6:26; Jas. 5:18). This is the heaven where birds fly. The second heaven is the stellar outer space where planets and stars are located (see Gen. 15:5; Matt. 24:29). The third heaven describes where God is located—the abode of God (see 2 Cor. 12:2). While heaven is a real place, not a lot is known about it other than that it is a place of joy, peace and continual worship of God.

One of the strongest arguments that heaven is a real place is the physical body of Jesus. Jesus was born of a virgin (see Isa. 7:14); He grew in physical, social and spiritual stature (see Luke 2:52); and He walked on this earth. Then, Jesus died a physical death on the cross.

That same human body that hung on the cross, however, was the resurrected body that came out of the grave on the third day. Since deity and humanity are insolubly united into one single Person, the Lord Jesus Christ, you cannot say that His soul went to heaven while His body did not. No! In His ascension, Jesus "passed through the heavens" (Heb. 4:14), meaning He went through the first and second heaven into the abode of God, which is the third heaven. "[He] ascended far above all the heavens" (Eph. 4:10).

Throughout all eternity, Christ will have a physical body: "But this man, because he continueth ever" (Heb. 7:24, *KJV*). Therefore, there must be a real heaven where a real physical Christ dwells throughout all eternity. There must be a real heaven, because Paul said that he was "caught up to the third heaven" (see 2 Cor. 12:1-4).

Paul describes himself in the third person saying, "He was caught up into Paradise and heard inexpressible words, which it is not lawful for a man to utter" (2 Cor. 12:4). This meant that Paul could not completely express in human words everything he saw in heaven. Also, God didn't want him to tell anyone about this experience. As a result, God gave Paul a physical problem so that he would be constantly reminded not to tell anyone what he saw, "Lest I should be exalted above measure by the abundance of the revelations, a thorn in the flesh was given to me . . . to buffet me, lest I be exalted above measure" (2 Cor. 12:7).

As great as was the third heaven that Paul saw, technically that will not be the place where we will spend eternity. John speaks about a fourth heaven when he said, "The first heaven and the first earth had passed away" (Rev. 21:1). We will live in a "new heaven and a new earth" (Rev. 21:1).

The key to understanding heaven is that word "new." This means that heaven will be more than new in time or sequence; it will be new in substance. The present material earth and heaven will not be annihilated, but will be transformed. The great Bible teacher and pastor of Moody Memorial Church, Harry Ironside, said, "Heaven will not be that unlike life here on earth."[1] As such, it'll have dirt, trees growing in it, streams and streets of gold.

The story is told of a millionaire who kept all his treasures in gold bullion. He didn't trust banks, stocks or life insurance. He prayed constantly throughout his life for God to let him take his gold coins and bars to heaven when he went. Finally, an angel told the Father, "He wants to bring his gold coins and bars with him."

The Father answered, "Why does he want to bring things that we make streets out of?"

Remember what the Bible says, "The heavens will pass away . . . both the earth and the works that are in it will be burned up" (2 Pet. 3:10). This means that the present heaven and earth will be burned up and transformed into something that is wholly new.

Prophecy-Preaching Churches

In the past 150 years, certain churches were known for prophetic teaching-preaching. Some would construct large dispensational posters; a few itinerate Bible teachers were able to take their charts with them to teach their messages in other churches.[2]

Pastor John Hagee, of Cornerstone Church in San Antonio, Texas, has brought prophetic preaching into the twenty-first century. He uses large artistic, multicolored charts to illustrate his prophetic sermons preached over a national network of television stations. Many of his sermon topics center on future events on earth. But verbal communication of a prophetic message is only the beginning; he has written best-selling books on how to interpret prophecy to today's developments in the Near East. Those titles are:

Financial Armageddon: We Are in a Battle for Our Very Survival, 2008

The Apocalypse Code: Find Out What the Bible Says About the End Times, 2007

In Defense of Israel, 2007

Jerusalem Countdown, 2007

The Battle for Jerusalem, 2003

From Daniel to Doomsday, 2000

Final Dawn over Jerusalem, 1999

The Hope of Heaven

The greatest thing about heaven is the hope given to those who plan to go there. Obviously, everyone wants to go to heaven, but no one wants to go through the pain and suffering that involves getting there. Everyone has a secret desire in his heart to go to heaven through the Rapture, even as John prayed: "Even so, come, Lord Jesus!" (Rev. 22:20). That way they can bypass pain and death, and go straight to heaven.

The word "hope" does not mean something that we wish for or have deep desire for; rather, the word "hope" comes from God Himself who gives the believer the absolute *assurance* that he will go to heaven.

In the Old Testament the psalmist could say, "My hope is in You" (Ps. 39:7). The same thing could be said of the New Testament, "The hope that is in you" (1 Pet. 3:15). John describes the same thing: "Everyone who has this hope in Him" (1 John 3:3). This hope is something that is born of God,

"Now may the God of hope fill you with all joy and peace in believing, that you may abound in hope by the power of the Holy Spirit" (Rom. 15:13). Notice the process: God gives the believer hope, who then reverses the action and puts his hope back in God. "I have hope in God" (Acts 24:15), said Paul.

The hope of the believer is in contrast to the unsaved person who has no hope (see Eph. 2:12; 1 Thess. 4:13). The hope that a Christian has is the result of his reciprocal relationship with Jesus Christ. A Christian's hope is not just wishful thinking that he might live with God after death. No, God has promised to be with him in this life and give him a new life when he enters heaven. The believer can be as sure of heaven as if he were already there.

So why do we have hope? Our hope grows out of our salvation, because we were given eternal life when we were saved (see Titus 1:2; 3:7); because our salvation is secure (see 1 Thess. 5:8);

and because we will meet Christ at His appearance (see Titus 2:13) and our bodies will be resurrected (see Acts 23:6; 26:6-7). Finally, we have hope because we know that our bodies will be transformed to live with God forever (see Phil. 3:21; 1 Cor. 15:51-59). Hope keeps us from becoming discouraged or disappointed, thus it is called the "anchor of the soul" (see Heb. 6:18-20).

What would happen to the Christian if he didn't have hope? He might give up during trials and sufferings; he might "throw in the towel" or, even worse, he might give up his faith. Hope keeps a Christian going even in the midst of trials and tribulations.

A Description of Heaven

The beauty and splendor of heaven far outshines anything that the human mind can comprehend. So, to communicate to man what heaven is like, God has used earthly treasures to describe heaven. It will be a huge, colorful city far beyond anything man could comprehend.

We read of "all kinds of precious stones" (see Rev. 21:19-20), and beautiful gates that are made of pearls (see Rev. 21:12-13), and walls that are made of jasper and a city that is made of pure gold (see Rev. 21:18). In heaven there is a River of Life, and a Tree of Life (see Rev. 22:1-2), and there is no need of sun or moon: "the city had no need of the sun or of the moon to shine in it, for the glory of God illuminated it. The Lamb is its light" (Rev. 21:23). Heaven obviously will be the most beautiful city ever seen by man.

The greatest quality of heaven is the fact that God will be there. John said, "I saw no temple in it, for the Lord God

Almighty and the Lamb are its temple" (Rev. 21:22). Remember, the word "temple" is symbolic of the presence of God, so the book of Revelation states, "Behold, the tabernacle of God is with men, and He will dwell with them" (Rev. 21:3). Just as in the Old Testament the Shekinah glory cloud came down upon the Tabernacle and God dwelt in the Tabernacle, so in heaven we have the symbolic presence of God, because heaven is described as a place "having the glory of God" (Rev. 21:11).

What Is Missing from Heaven?

Tears	Rev. 12:1	Defilement	Rev. 21:27
Death	Rev. 21:4	Abomination	Rev. 21:27
Sorrow	Rev. 21:4	Curses	Rev. 22:3
Crying	Rev. 21:4	Liars	Rev. 21:27
Pain	Rev. 21:4	Sun	Rev. 21:23
Night	Rev. 21:25	Moon	Rev. 21:23

The flip side of heaven is that it has no disappointments, failures or regrets. "And God will wipe away every tear from their eyes; there shall be no more death, nor sorrow, nor crying. There shall be no more pain, for the former things have passed away" (Rev. 21:4).

Years ago, I was teaching a lesson in the Auditorium Bible Class on the topic, "What Will We Do in Heaven?" I mentioned to a secretary at Liberty University that in heaven she would see her former husband who had divorced her. Then with great bitterness, she said, "That sucker won't be there . . ."

Her statement reveals the bitterness of divorce here on this earth, but the Bible tells us that if both he and she were in heaven, there would be no tears, no bitterness, no acrimony.

Have you ever thought how our interests and attitudes toward heaven change throughout our Christian life? When we are young, most of us think about heaven as a place that is far off. In our young life we think about dedicating our life to God, serving Him and how we could glorify Him on this earth. We live an active Christian life and seldom think of life after the grave.

As we get older, we come closer to moving into heaven, so we think of it differently. The older Christian wants to know more about details of what heaven is like, what they will do there and the quality of life in heaven itself. The closer you get to heaven, the more real it becomes. But in the final analysis, the destination of heaven is not as important as the fact that we will live with God for all eternity.

Hope is one of the most powerful motivations known to mankind, and hope on this earth transforms individuals and changes society. People with hope live confident lives and inspire others to live the same way.

The church offers more than hope after death; it offers reasons why people should live godly lives now in preparation for the next life.

What's right with the church? The enduring hope it offers is a prime motivation that enriches life and makes it worthwhile.

What's right with the church? Heaven!

Epilogue

Christianity began when a man named Jesus—the Eternal Word of God—became flesh and lived among us. Jesus had a physical body that at times was hungry, became tired and as other humans, grew to full manhood. While in His physical body, Jesus was limited by His humanity; He had to eat and sleep, and He died nailed to a cross.

On the other side of the issue was His deity; Jesus was God. As deity, He possessed God's attributes and had supernatural power to do miracles. As the Son of God, Jesus did not sin. God could not die, yet the threat of death awaited Him in His flesh.

So He died for the sins of the world. In His unique physical body, Jesus arose from the dead because He was both deity and human. As such, He lived again in the flesh. He is the God-man.

Today, the physical body of Jesus is sitting in heaven at the right hand of God the Father. That's the body that every Christian identifies with because they died with Christ, were buried with Christ and were raised again with Him (see Rom. 6:5-6; Eph. 2:4-6).

But here's the mystery. The local church on earth, which is called His Body, is a reflection of the divine body in heaven. Both are a God-thing and a human-thing. The body of Jesus in heaven is made up of all who are "in Christ." The local church is made up of human people and, as such, the local church is subject to the limitations of humanity. But at the same time, a local church has some aspects of divinity because each believing member is indwelt by Jesus Christ (see Gal. 2:20).

The local church—just like Jesus' physical body on earth—gets tired, makes mistakes and stumbles. Just as Jesus Christ in the human body was the God-man, so the church is both a living organism and a human organization.

When you criticize the local church—the human organization—remember that its members get bogged down in committees, do stupid things and are driven by their pride, prejudices and, yes, their sins.

When you praise the local church, remember that Christ works through members who sacrifice their time, treasure and talents to serve other people. They experience the power of Christ who helps them overcome bad habits and selfish inclinations to live lives that exalt God.

There are plenty of reasons to criticize the local church, and it seems at the beginning of the twenty-first century that there are a lot more criticisms of the church then there are compliments. Perhaps the church is failing, but in each past century there have been all types of failures. Nothing's new.

This book looks at the good things about the local church. It discusses *what's right with the church*. We've looked at the eternal principles that God ordained for His people corporately. We like what we see, and we realize that life being what it is, the church is constituted—or it should be—to do God's work in the world.

If every church were perfect and if its people were perfect, people would flock to the church for the wrong reason. They would seek utopia, and not Christ. They would worship perfection, and not the Father.

So what must the church be? The church of sinful—yet saved—people will attract sinful people. Why? Because the world will see that the people of God in a church have faced the same problems as they and have overcome their limitations to bring them to Christ who saved them. The church must be what it is— a group of sinful people who live victorious over sin—so they can attract unsaved people to Christ.

The plan is so simple, but it's also grand because there is profundity in simplicity. What's right with the church? It's a place for sinners who have been redeemed by Christ to attract others so they, too, can be redeemed by Christ. When the church remembers who it is and where its members have come from, it can be the right place for God to continue to work in lives.

WHAT IS A CHURCH?

As we see some churches dying, we also see other local churches growing in size and strength. We see some new churches being planted, while others close their doors and die. Why are some churches strong and others weak? What makes a "good" church? And what's a "dying" church?

Theological issues are either covered by neglect or there is no pressing need to determine what God's Word says on a particular doctrine. But once an issue becomes the focus of controversy, good men examine it carefully, disagree passionately and finally exhaust every shade of meaning. Thereafter the issue still divides good men, but at least the implications of the doctrine are understood.

Each past generation has fought its own theological battles. The theological battle of the past century concerned itself with the Word of God: What is inspiration and inerrancy? Before that, the issue was eschatology: When is the Lord coming?

The doctrine of the local church is today's theological battleground. It is the burning issue that separates Christians today. Inasmuch as we live in a pluralistic society, people project their needs and ideas for the church. Each one from a different background devises a different concept of what the church should be. The pages of the New Testament must be carefully read to determine the makeup of a church.

Of course a church is not the building, nor is any gathering of Christians a church just because they call themselves by that title. What is the *ecclesia*? The word *ecclesia* in the New Testament meant "gathering," and any church must be a gathering of those who are Christians. The term *ecclesia*, mentioned 114 times in the New Testament, could have been better translated in our Bible as "assembly." Whenever we think of the term "church," let us always primarily concern ourselves with the people who are assembled in the name of the Lord.

A Church Is an Assembly of Believers

The first criterion for a New Testament church is an assembly of those who agree by statement of faith, or by affirmation of the church, that they would be part of that church.

> A church is an assembly of believers in whom Christ dwells, under the discipline of the Word of God, organized for evangelism, education, fellowship and worship, administering the ordinances and reflecting the spiritual gifts.

On the day of Pentecost, those who were saved were immediately baptized and were added to the church. In their baptism they affirmed their salvation and asked to be part of those who followed Christ. "Then those who gladly received his word were baptized; and that day about three thousand souls were added to them" (Acts 2:41).

Baptism became more than an initiatory rite into a local church; it is a symbol portraying the ultimate meaning of the Lord's death. The church is the Body of Christ (see Eph. 1:22-

23). When He hung on Calvary, sinners were placed into the Body of Christ, and when Christ suffered vicariously, the penalty of their sins was propitiated because they were in Jesus Christ. Individuals were identified with Christ in His death, burial and resurrection (see Rom. 6:4-6). And, as a result, when Christ died, believers died with Him: "I have been crucified with Christ; it is no longer I who live, but Christ lives in me" (Gal. 2:20).

There will be some in the church who are not saved, as was the case in New Testament times (see Acts 8:13-23). However, all should be accepted into the church upon their profession of faith. The church is an assembly of believers, and when the church is made up of unbelievers, it is no longer a New Testament church.

The Unique Presence of Jesus Christ Dwells in a Church

Christ is the light of the world (see John 8:12). The primary purpose of the church is to hold up the light in a dark, perverse world (see Phil. 2:15-16). The church is more than an organization; it is an organism, and its life is Christ. He dwells in the midst of His people. "For where two or three are gathered together in My name, I am there in the midst of them" (Matt. 18:20).

Christ walked through the seven churches in the book of Revelation and commended them for their good works (see Rev. 2:3) and rebuked them for their sin and false doctrine (see Rev. 2:1,3; 2:20; 3:1). When Christ rebuked the churches in the book of Revelation, He threatened to take away their candlestick (see Rev. 2:5), which would have been removing His presence from the people. When Christ is removed from a New

Testament church, it is similar to the Shekinah glory cloud leaving the Old Testament Temple. If a group of people do not have Jesus Christ dwelling in their midst, they are no longer a New Testament church.

A Church Must Be Under the Discipline of the Word of God

One of the first religious exercises of the New Testament church after the day of Pentecost was that "they continued steadfastly in the apostles' doctrine and fellowship" (Acts 2:42).

Doctrinal purity is essential for a New Testament church. There is a unique union between Christ and the Bible—both are the Word of God. "In the beginning was the Word, and the Word was with God, and the Word was God" (John 1:1). Christ pointed men to the Word of God, for it was their only way to obtain eternal life (see John 6:63).

When an organizational problem came up in the Early Church, the apostles realized they could not waste time waiting on tables when they should be giving themselves to the Word of God (see Acts 6:4). A local church must place itself under the authority of God by placing itself under the discipline of the Word of God.

When the minister gives a positive proclamation of the Word of God, this is positive discipline, leading to correct life and belief. When the minister rebukes a congregation for their sin, this is negative discipline, just as a parent rebukes a child for going too near the fire. The purpose of discipline is the positive growth and negative correction of the child. The purpose of discipline by the Word of God is the positive growth and negative correction of the New Testament church. When an assembly of people removed themselves from under the authority of the Word of God, they ceased being a New Testament church.

A Church Must Be Organized for Evangelism, Education, Worship and Fellowship

The purpose of a church is more than a "back-slapping fellowship" of mutual friends. In the Early Church they "did not cease teaching and preaching Jesus as the Christ" (Acts 5:42). Since the church believed that everyone was lost, it also believed that everyone must receive an honest hearing of the gospel. The church in Jerusalem carried the gospel to every home so that its persecutors could say, "You have filled Jerusalem with your doctrine" (Acts 5:28). The early disciples were carrying out the Great Commission. The first obligation upon a church is evangelism.

The second requirement was education; it had to indoctrinate the new Christians into the faith so they would live for Christ. The last part of the Great Commission reinforced this belief: "teaching them to observe all things that I have commanded you" (Matt. 28:20). Next, the New Testament church both provides fellowship and becomes a place for mutual interaction. John 1–2 set fellowship as a standard for Christian behavior. Finally, worship is required of all Christians. Jesus said, "The true worshipers will worship the Father in spirit and truth" (John 4:23). The entire book of Psalms gives the Christian the example of worship.

The marks of a New Testament church are evangelism, education, fellowship and worship. When a church neglects these ministries, it abdicates its calling.

A Church Administers the Ordinances

Two ordinances were given to the church: baptism and the Lord's Table (or Supper). These are to be celebrated by the church when it assembles together. Even though the ordinances are given for personal edification and testimony, an individual does not partake of these apart from the church.

Baptism reflects one's testimony of conversion, that a person is identified with Christ in His death, burial and resurrection. This spiritual identification with Christ on the cross is reflected by one's identification with Christ's Body on earth, the church. The Lord's Table is a means of edification, fellowship and personal introspection. A believer is to examine himself before partaking. God provided the Lord's Table to keep His church pure and separated from the world.

A Church Reflects the Spiritual Gifts

Not every group of Christians is destined to grow into a church. A group of people must be properly baptized, under the Word of God and organized for God's priorities. God then raises up leadership to bring the church into existence. These leaders must have the "spiritual gifts" (see 1 Cor. 12; Rom. 12; Eph. 4). God gives gifted men to a church, and when the leaders appear, it is an indication that God wants the people to organize into a New Testament church. "And God has appointed these in the church: first apostles, second prophets, third teachers" (1 Cor. 12:28). "He Himself gave some to be apostles, some prophets, some evangelists, and some pastors and teachers" (Eph. 4:11). When an organization ceases to have spiritual leadership, it ceases to function as a New Testament church.

ENDNOTES

Introduction: What's Right with the Church

1. "New Study Shows Trends in Tithing and Donating," The Barna Group, April 14, 2008. http://www.barna.org/barna-update/article/18-congregations/41-new-study-shows-trends-in-tithing-and-donating (accessed June 2009).

2. George Barna, *Revolution* (Wheaton, IL: Tyndale House Publishers, 2006). The author continually points out the weaknesses of the present-day church as a basis for his ideas of new innovations and methods that must be used to bring about a revolution.

Chapter 1: When the Church Is Right on Jesus

1. Charles R. Biggs, "Important Creeds and Councils of the Christian Church," 2003. http://www.aplacefortruth.org/creeds9.htm (accessed June 2009).

2. Elmer L. Towns, *The Names of Jesus* (Denver, CO: Accent Publications, 1989), p. 15.

Chapter 2: When the Church Is Right on the Bible

1. Chuck Smith began Calvary Chapel in 1966, and today it averages more than 22,000 weekly in attendance. There are more than 800 churches that fellowship in the Calvary Chapel network of churches, and most of their pastors preach through the Bible verse by verse.

2. The average attendance of this Calvary Chapel is more than 10,000 weekly.

3. Chuck Smith, *Calvary Chapel Distinctives: The Foundational Principles of the Calvary Chapel Movement* (Costa Mesa, CA: The Word for Today Publishers, 2004), p. 59.

4. Ibid.

5. Ibid., p. 60.

6. Michael R. Tucker, *The Church That Dared to Change* (Wheaton, IL: Tyndale House, 1975), p. 12.

7. Gary Inrig, *Life in His Body* (Wheaton, IL: Harold Shaw, 1975), p. 43.

8. "John MacArthur's Questions and Answers," Bible Bulletin Board. http://www.biblebb.com/macqa.htm (accessed February 2009).

9. Tucker, *The Church That Dared to Change*, p. 14.

10. Dan Baumann, *All Originality Makes a Dull Church* (Santa Ana, CA: Vision House, 1976), p. 45.

11. Wycliffe Bible Translators website, www.wycliffe.org (accessed January 2009).

12. Ibid.

13. See chapter 3 for a complete story of my conversion.

Chapter 3: When the Church Is Right on Conversion

1. I attended Eastern Heights Presbyterian Church in Savannah, Georgia. To see a complete story of this church and its influence on me, see my Doctor of Ministry dissertation at www.elmertowns.com, under resources/biography/analysis of the gift of faith.

2. http://dictionary.reference.com/browse/conversion, s.v. "conversion" (accessed January 2009).

3. I attended the funeral of Dr. Kennedy and was amazed at the vast number of people who testified they had found Christ when someone from the church came to their home and led them to Christ.

4. Thom Rainer documents his research on evangelism in the church in the following works: *Essential Church: Reclaiming a Generation of Dropouts* (with Sam S. Rainer) (Nashville, TN: Broadman & Holman), 2008; *Simple Church: Returning to God's Process for Making Disciples* (with Eric Geiger) (Nashville, TN: Broadman & Holman), 2006; *Effective Evangelistic Churches* (Nashville, TN: Broadman & Holman, 1996).

5. Thom S. Rainer and Sam S. Rainer III, "Wanted: More Evangelistic Churches," *Outreach*, January/February 2007. http://outreachmagazine.com/library/insights/ JF07RainerMoreEvangelisticChurches.asp (accessed January 2009).

6. Ibid.

7. Ibid.

Chapter 4: When the Church Is Right on Sin

1. *Dictionary.com*, s.v. "sin." http://dictionary.reference.com/browse/SIN (accessed February 2009).

2. "Shoplifting Is Stealing: Alarming Facts About Shoplifting." http://www.shop liftingisstealing.com (accessed February 2009).

3. "Trends in Felony Crime in Washington State and Related Taxpayer Costs," *Washington State Institute for Public Policy*, 1997 data. http://www.wsipp.wa.gov/rptfiles/ crime_trend99.pdf (accessed February 2009).

4. John Witte Jr., "Sex May Be Free, but Children Come with a Cost We Must Accept," *Atlanta Journal-Constitution*. http://www.ajc.com/search/content/opinion/ stories/2008/08/10/witted.html (accessed February 2009).

5. Amanda Terkel, "Fact-Checking Conservative Outrage Over STD Prevention Provision in Economic Recovery Package," Think Progress, January 28, 2009. http://thinkprogress.org/2009/01/28/drudge-std/ (accessed February 2009).

6. Gregory L. Jantz with Ann McMurray, *Turning the Tables on Gambling: Help and Hope for an Addictive Behavior* (Colorado Springs, CO: WaterBrook Press, 2001), excerpt from "Dr. Jantz's "Overcoming Gambling," http://www.overcominggambling.com/ facts.html#Statistics (accessed February 2009).

7. "Cigarette Smoking and Cardiovascular Diseases," American Heart Association, May 18, 2009. http://www.americanheart.org/presenter.jhtml?identifier=4545 (accessed February 2009).

8. "The Impact of Alcohol Abuse on American Society," Alcoholics Victorious, article reprinted from *Rescue Magazine*, Winter 1994. http://www.alcoholicsvictorious.org/ faq/impact.html (accessed February 2009).

9. Ibid.

10. "The Alcohol Cost Calculator for Business: The Facts About the Impact of Problem Drinking," The George Washington University Medical Center. http://www.alco holcostcalculator.org/business/cost/?page=1 (accessed February 2009).

11. Ibid.

12. "The Impact of Alcohol Abuse on American Society," Alcoholics Victorious. http://www.alcoholicsvictorious.org/faq/impact.html (accessed February 2009).

13. Ibid.

14. Ibid.

15. Rich Branch, "Christian Science Explains . . . Jesus Never Died, for No One Sinned! Believer's Web, April 25, 2003. http://www.believersweb.org/view.cfm?ID=589 (accessed February 2009). According to Mary Baker Eddy, founder of the First Church of Christ, Scientist, commonly known as Christian Science, Jesus could

not die for man's sins, because mankind never sinned! Despite the fact that the Bible is explicit about man's sinful nature, that Jesus came to save man from sin by becoming the sacrifice for man, and that this saving process involved the death, burial and resurrection of Jesus, Christian Science explains this as error—or at the very least—man's interpretation on these events are in error.

16. Elmer L. Towns, *Theology for Today* (Fort Worth, TX: Harcourt and Brace, 2000), pp. 499-500.

Chapter 5: When the Church Is Right in an Ongoing Relationship with God

1. There is no condemnation to those who are "in Christ" (see Rom. 8:1). If any man is "in Christ," he is a new creature (see 2 Cor. 5:17). Paul declared that he had been crucified and that Christ lived in him (see Gal. 2:20). We are baptized "into Christ" (see Gal. 3:27). Christ dwells in the heart by faith (see Eph. 3:17). We are created "in Christ Jesus unto good works" (Eph. 2:10).

2. The phrase "the heavenlies" is the key phrase in the book of Ephesians, and it stands for all the blessings that the believer has in Christ. He should "walk worthy" in his life on this earth because of all the things that God has for him in heaven.

3. Edward E. Hindson, *Glory in the Church* (Nashville, TN: Thomas Nelson, Inc., Publishers, 1975), see Postscript, pp. 118–126.

4. Elmer L. Towns and Douglas Porter, *The Ten Greatest Revivals Ever* (Ann Arbor, MI: Servant Publications, 2000).

5. The order of *The Ten Greatest Revivals Ever* was determined by the following who read the manuscript: Bill Bright, Gerald Brooks, David Yonggi Cho, Robert Coleman, James O. Davis, Lewis Drummond, Dale Galloway, Eddie Gibbs, Jack Hayford, Charles Kelly, D. James Kennedy, Ron Phillips, Alvin Reid, Chuck Smith, Tommy Tenney, C. Peter Wagner, and Steve Wingfield.

Chapter 6: When the Church Is Right on Worship

1. Elmer L. Towns, *10 of Today's Most Innovative Churches* (Ventura, CA: Regal Books, 1990). See chapter 3, "A Reformation of Worship: The Church On The Way, Van Nuys, California."

2. Ibid., pp. 60-72.

3. Jack Hayford, *Worship His Majesty* (Ventura, CA: Regal Books, 2000).

4. See www.thedream.c3church.org (accessed February 2009).

5. "C3 Church," Practical Worship Blogspot.com, September 6, 2007. http://practical worship.blogspot.com/2007/09/c3-church.html (accessed February 2009).

6. The word "worship" comes from an old Scottish term "worth-ship." So the worshiper must recognize the biblical "worth" of God in his worship.

7. Elmer Towns, "Effective Evangelism View," in Gary McIntosh, *Evaluating the Church Growth Movement (5 Views)* (Grand Rapids, MI: Zondervan, 2004), p. 48.

8. See www.libertybaptistfellowship.com and www.namb.net.

9. Elmer Towns, general editor, *A Practical Encyclopedia of Evangelism and Church Growth* (Ventura, CA: Regal Books, 1996). See "Church Growth Movement, Beginning of," p. 76; and "Church Growth Definitions," p. 72.

Chapter 7: When the Church Is Right as an Interactive Fellowship

1. "Christianity Is No Longer Americans' Default Faith," The Barna Group, January 12, 2009. http://www.barna.org/barna-update/article/12-faithspirituality/15-christianity-is-no-longer-americans-default-faith, (accessed April 2009).

2. Elmer Towns, C. Peter Wagner and Thom S. Rainer, *The Everychurch Guide to Growth* (Nashville, TN: Broadman and Holman Publishers, 1998), p. 151.

3. Research results from survey conducted by Elmer Towns for class at Trinity Evangelical Divinity School, Wheaton, Illinois, Spring 1967.

4. Elmer L. Towns, John N. Vaughan and David J. Seifert, *The Complete Book of Church Growth* (Wheaton, IL: Tyndale House Publishers, 1987), p. 62.

5. Ibid., p. 63.

Chapter 8: When the Church Is Right on Helping Needy People

1. "Lord Ashley," Spartacus Educational. http://www.spartacus.schoolnet.co.uk/ IRashley.htm (accessed January 2009).

2. "Elizabeth Fry," Everything2. http://everything2.com/e2node/Elizabeth%2520Fry, (accessed February 2009).

3. Michael Nazir-Ali, "Can Christians Practice Their Faith Publicly in Britain?" Diocese of Rochester, February 6, 2009. http://www.rochester.anglican.org/ pdf_files/bishop_michael_articles/060209_statement_christiian_practise.pdf (accessed June 2009).

4. Elmer L. Towns and Warren Bird, *Into the Future* (Grand Rapids, MI: Baker Book House, 2000), p. 56. This is the definition of servant evangelism.

5. Elmer L. Towns, general editor, *A Practical Encyclopedia: Evangelism and Church Growth* (Ventura, CA: Regal Books, 1995), p. 218.

Chapter 9: When the Church Is Right on the Family

1. Cathy Meyer, "The Issue of No-Fault Divorce," About.com. http://divorce support.about.com/od/maritalproblems/i/nofault_fault_2.htm (accessed April 2009).

2. Jerry Strite, "Raising a G-Rated Family in an R-Rated World," sermon delivered in May 2006. http://www.sermoncentral.com/sermon.asp?SermonID=91301 (accessed May 2009).

3. Ibid.

4. Some sarcastic TV preachers who oppose homosexuality have said, "God created Adam and Eve. If God wanted homosexual relationships, he would have created Adam and Steve."

5. God planned sex for several reasons, among them to lead to procreation and the continuation of the human race. God knew the foundation of human society and culture was the nurturing, training and protection of children within the family.

6. The American Association of Christian Counselors is perhaps the largest organization in the United States, with more than 50,000 Christian counselors enrolled in its membership. See http://www.marriagecomission.com/organizations/?ID=19.

7. "Facts and Studies," Council for American Private Education, data from National Center for Education Statistics, 2007-2009. http://www.capenet.org/facts.html #FAQ (accessed May 2009).

8. "How Many Homeschoolers Are There?" FamilyEducation.com. http://school. familyeducation.com/home-schooling/alternative-education/56352.html (accessed April 2009). See also Greg Toppo, "Profound Shift in Home Schooling," *USA Today*, May 29, 2009. http://www.usatoday.com/news/education/2009-05-28-homeschooling_N.htm (accessed June 2009).

9. As I mentioned in chapter 7, the largest church in the world, the Full Gospel Church in Seoul, South Korea, has approximately 65,000 cell groups meeting in homes throughout the city. Pastor David Yonggi Cho tells me that there are ap-

proximately 650,000 people in these groups. When I did research for the chapter on the house church movement in *11 Innovations in the Local Church* (Regal, 2008), I found conflicting accounts of how many house churches there are in America, from a low estimate of 1,000 to a high of 10,000. So, all we know about house churches is that we don't know how many there are in the United States, but their number seems to be growing.

Chapter 10: When the Church Is Right on Multiracial Involvement

1. "Bridgeway Community Church: History." http://www.bridgewayonline.org/About_Bridgeway/?p=histor, (accessed January 2009).
2. Ibid.
3. David Anderson, *Multicultural Ministry: Finding Your Church's Unique Rhythm* (Grand Rapids, MI: Zondervan, 2004).
4. Elmer L. Towns, *The Everychurch Guide to Growth* (Nashville, TN: Broadman & Holman, 1998), p. 37.
5. Ibid., p. 190.
6. George A. Yancey, *One Body, One Spirit: Principles of Successful Multiracial Churches* (Downers Grove, IL: InterVarsity Press, 2003).
7. Pearl S. Buck, "Quotations on Education, Equity, and Multiculturalism," compiled by Paul C. Gorski for EdChange and the Multicultural Pavilion. http://www.edchange.org/multicultural/ (accessed February 2009).
8. "Charles R. Drew," Wikipedia.com http://en.wikipedia.org/wiki/Charles_Drew (accessed February 2009).

Chapter 11: When the Church Is Right on the Great Commission

1. Elmer Towns, *Core Christianity* (Chattanooga, TN: AMG Publishers, 2007), p. 133.
2. Ibid., p. 134.
3. "Constantine's Conversion," *New World Encyclopedia.* http://www.newworldencyclopedia.org/entry/Constantine_I#Constantine.27s_conversion (accessed February 2009).
4. "Coming of Christianity to Ireland," WesleyJohnson.com. http://www.wesleyjohnston.com/users/ireland/past/pre_norman_history/christianity.html (accessed February 2009.
5. "John Calvin," History Learning Site. http://www.historylearningsite.co.uk/John_Calvin.htm (accessed February 2009).
6. Elmer Towns and Douglas Porter, *The Ten Greatest Revivals Ever* (Ann Arbor, MI: Servant Publications, 2000), pp. 83-86.
7. Elmer Towns, *The Christian Hall of Fame* (Grand Rapids, MI: Baker Book House, 1971), p. 190.
8. "Bill Bright Author Page," The Steve Laube Agency. http://www.stevelaube.com/authors/billbright.htm (accessed February 2009).
9. "Oswald Jeffrey Smith, Pastor, Evangelist," Believer's Web, March 17, 2003. http://www.believersweb.org/view.cfm?id=130&rc=1&list=multi (accessed February 2009).

Chapter 12: When the Church Is Right on the Future

1. H. A. Ironside, "Care for God's Fruit-Trees . . . The Father's House and the Way There," *Wholesome Words.* http://www.wholesomewords.org/etexts/ironside/care10.html (accessed February 2009).
2. Clarence Larkin, "Dispensational Charts." http://www.preservedwords.com/charts.htm (accessed February 2009).